Tent,
Canvas
& Webbing Repair

Tent, Canvas & Webbing Repair

MAINTENANCE MANUAL FOR THE OUTDOORSMAN

Drake Publishers Inc
New York • London

Photographs on pages ix-xii by R. E. Smallman, GSUSA, from
Tents and Simple Shelters © 1973 Girl Scouts of the U.S.A.

Published in 1978 by
Drake Publishers, Inc.
801 Second Avenue
New York, N.Y. 10017

Library of Congress Cataloging in Publication Data

Drake Publishers.
    Tent, canvas, and webbing repair.

    Bibliography: p.
    1. Tents — Maintenance and repair. 2. Canvas —
Maintenance and repair. I. Title.
TS1860.D7   1978   658'.53   77-88955
ISBN 0-8473-1658-0

Printed in the United States of America

CONTENTS

WHAT EVERY CAMPER SHOULD KNOW

The more a tent is used — or gives service, if you like — the more it will require certain measures of maintenance and repair. In this way its service life is extended and the quality of its usefulness to tenters and campers is maintained at a high level. This is true not only of tents, but of other camping gear — sleeping bags, packs, carrying straps, and so on — as well. Thus, obviously, knowledge of maintenance and repair techniques is of considerable importance to the outdoorsman.

Such knowledge must include a familiarity with ropes and knots, pegs, grommets, fasteners, rivets, tacks, and other hardware. And it should extend to sewing techniques and methods of patching the fabrics, whether canvas or nylon. It is perhaps not necessary to say that the one fundamental rule of proper maintenance is to keep tents, canvas, and webbing as clean as possible in the field, and to clean the evidence of use before it is stored away for use in the future. As a corollary, this requires inspection of the gear before it is stored: repairs should be made at that time. As an introduction to such necessary knowledge, the outdoorsman might start by considering the pictures on the following pages.

Ease of maintenance and repair is one reason why the standard wall tent is favored for long-term camping. The one shown above is made of cotton duck, a particularly easy material for patching, which comes in 9½, 12 and 16 foot squares. Roll-up flaps and sides not only provide air space between the tent and fly for coolness, but also are easily accessible for most basic maintenance measures.

(Photograph by R.E. Smallman, courtesy of Girl Scouts of U.S.A.)

It is important to bear in mind that cotton tent materials and hemp ropes shrink when they get wet. Thus a basic maintenance step is the loosening of guy ropes in the rain in order to prevent ripping. Sliding metal or wood tighteners simplify this procedure.
(Photograph R. E. Smallman, courtesy Girl Scouts of U.S.A.)

When selecting tenting material, bear in mind that heavy canvas duck is not completely waterproof. However, it does "breathe" to prevent condensation inside. A periodic check should be made of grommets used with this gear as they may pull out from too great a strain and then have to be replaced along with, quite possibly, patching or repairing the fabric.
(Photograph by R. E. Smallman, courtesy of Girl Scouts of U.S.A.)

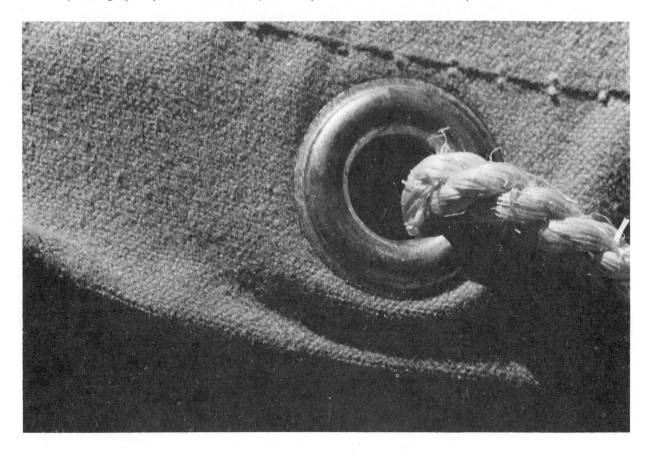

All chapes, straps and ties are designed and sewn to bear the strain that will be placed on them. This applies to those used on large, sturdy tents, and small lightweight tents as well.
(Photograph by R. E. Smallman, courtesy of Girl Scouts of U.S.A.)

Tent,
Canvas
& Webbing Repair

CHAPTER 1

INTRODUCTION

1. Purpose

This manual gives information on the general repair of tents, canvas, and webbing. Much of this information is also applicable to general repair of upholstery. The information, which applies to both mobile and fixed repair units or installations, is for the use of trained personnel.

2. Scope

This manual includes common procedures for inspecting and marking items for repair, repair procedures, and procedures for inspecting the finished repairs. Technical manuals on special-purpose tents give detailed information for repairing these tents.

CHAPTER 2
STANDARDS OF REPAIR

3. Tents and Heavy Canvas

The following standards govern the repair of tents and heavy canvas:

a. Canvas.

(1) Faded tent canvas is acceptable provided the fading is the only defect.

(2) Canvas with holes, tears, badly worn areas, weak spots, and frayed sections must be repaired.

(3) Spotted and stained canvas showing deterioration when thumb tested must be repaired (para 39a). Nondeteriorating spots and stains caused by mildew, sap, and dirt are acceptable provided the canvas has been brushed clean.

(4) A badly damaged section or one containing a large number of patches must be replaced with a new section similar to that in the original construction.

(5) Previous repairs of substandard quality are defects and must be properly repaired.

b. Stitching and Seams.

(1) Breaks and runoffs of stitching must be repaired.

(2) Seams in which the thread has rotted must be restitched.

c. Hardware.

(1) Rusty, corroded, bent, broken, or otherwise defective hardware must be replaced.

(2) Hardware having an electro-zinc-plate finish must be replaced with hardware having a hot-galvanized finish.

Note. Electro-zinc-plated hardware has a dull, flaky finish, whereas, hot-galvanize-finished hardware has a bright, nonflaky finish.

d. Webbing. Defective tie tapes, wall lines, ring and snap chapes, corner straps, and webbing reinforcements must be replaced and stitched as in the original construction.

e. Lines.

(1) Frayed or raveled ends must be hand whipped or machine stitched.

(2) Lines with frayed or broken strands must be replaced. Serviceable lines taken from unserviceable items may be used for this purpose.

f. Other Repairs.

(1) When a ventilator opening has more than two patches or defects, the entire ventilator section must be replaced.

(2) A ventilator cover with more than two patches or defects must be replaced with a serviceable cover.

(3) A blackout flap not forming a good closure must be detached and replaced, making certain the replacement flap covers the old needle holes.

(4) Fabric to replace a sash pocket should be cut larger than the original pocket piece in order to cover the exposed needle holes.

(5) An extension cloth causing the tent to wrinkle must be replaced.

(6) A ventilator duct with a hole or tear may be patched with either a sewn patch or a cement patch.

(7) A window flap of improper dimensions must be replaced with a serviceable flap of proper dimensions.

(8) A window framework assembly may be patched, provided the patching does not distort the window opening.

(9) A window sash made of cellulose acetate and cotton netting must be replaced with a flexible waterproof-film sash.

(10) An outlet sash may be patched or repaired, provided the proper size is maintained and the number of patches does not exceed three.

(11) An excessively stretched rope reinforcement may be repaired by shortening it and restitching it as in the original construction, or it may be replaced with a new rope.

(12) A stovepipe opening that is extensively burned must be cut out from seam to seam and replaced with a serviceable opening.

4. Equipment Other Than Tents and Heavy Canvas

Standards of repair for canvas and webbing items other than tents and heavy-canvas items are given in technical manuals for the items. These manuals should be consulted before repairs are made.

CHAPTER 3

BASIC REPAIR

5. Tentage Repair Kit

The tentage repair kit (fig 1) is issued for the hand repair of canvas and webbing. It consists of a tentage repair kit case, tools, repair materials, and tent parts.

a. Adhesive. Tent-patching adhesive (1) is a solution of synthetic rubber. Normally, it can easily be applied to a fabric with a soft-bristle brush, a knife, or a flat object such as a wooden paddle. The adhesive is waterproof, flexible, and very cohesive. It is used to attach patches to damaged tents.

b. Beeswax. Technical beeswax (2) is applied to thread to keep it from fraying as it is pulled through material. It also makes thread pass more easily through heavy materials.

c. Repair Kit Case. The repair kit case (3, fig 1 and fig 2) has webbing handles and is

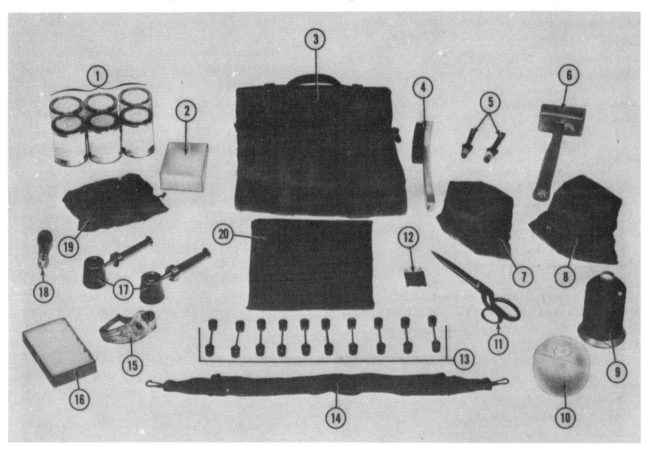

1	Adhesive	11	Bent trimmer's shears
2	Beeswax	12	Sailmaker's needles
3	Tentage repair kit case	13	Tent line slips
4	Wire brush	14	Carrying sling
5	Cutting punches	15	Sewing palm
6	Rawhide mallet	16	Slide-fastener lubricant
7	No. 4 brass grommets	17	Punch-and-die sets
8	No. 5 brass grommets	18	Saddler's sewing awl
9	Polyester thread	19	Connecting rings
10	Cotton wrapping twin, 5 ply	20	Cotton-duck cloth

Figure 1. Tentage repair kit.

constructed of heavy, olive-drab canvas. The case, which opens like a suitcase, is secured at the top by straps and buckles. Attached to one side of the case is a panel that can be unfolded several lengths. On the inside of the panel are pockets, each marked with a number so that tools can be easily located and replaced. The case has two compartments that differ in size and design. They are held together by the panel.

(1) *Large compartment.* The large compartment holds bulky tools, parts, and materials. Numbered sleeve pockets for stowing patching adhesives are at each end of the compartment. The large compartment also has three canvas bags with drawstrings, for stowing repair parts. The top of the compartment is covered by a canvas flap, secured by two webbing straps and buckles.

(2) *Small compartment.* The small compartment has pockets for holding tools. Bulky patching material is also stowed within the compartment. The top of the compartment is covered by a canvas flap, secured by snap fasteners.

d. Wire Brush. The wire brush (4, fig 1) is a hardwood handle with wire bristles at one end. The brush is used to remove dirt from tents before repairs are made.

e. Cutting Punches. The kit has two cutting punches. The 1/2-inch size (5) is used to cut the

No. 4 grommet hole, and the 9/16-inch size is used to cut the No. 5 grommet hole.

f. Mallet. The mallet (6) has a wooden handle and a rawhide head. The mallet is used to strike the grommet-setting dies and grommet hole cutters. The striking blow of the mallet is absorbed by its rawhide head, thereby increasing the life of the dies and cutters. A steel hammer should never be used because a sharp blow crystallizes the steel in the die or cutter.

g. Grommets. The repair kit contains No. 4 grommets (7) and No. 5 grommets (8). The No. 4 grommet has a 1/2-inch inside diameter; the No. 5 grommet has a 5/8-inch inside diameter. Grommets have two parts, a male part called a barrel and a female part called a washer. After they are positioned on opposite sides of a piece of material, the male and female parts are clinched together by a punch-and-die set. Grommets are used to reinforce and protect materials at those spots admitting a rope, a line, a spindle, or a webbing strap.

h. Thread. The kit has size FF, olive-drab polyester thread (9) that conforms to type I, class I, subclass B, Federal specification V–T–285a.

i. Twine. The kit has 1/2-pound balls of cotton wrapping twine (10, fig 1). The twine is used for sewing grommets by hand.

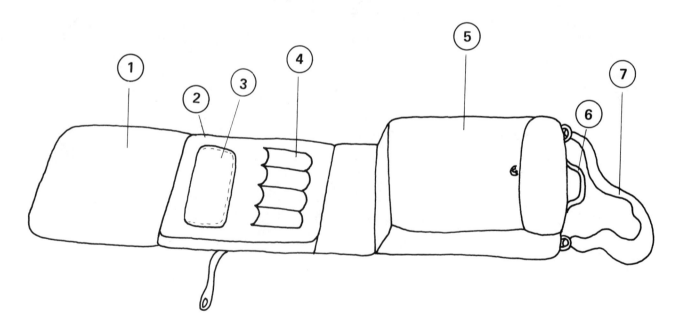

1 Flap to small compartment
2 Small compartment
3 Patch pocket for extra needles, and awl needle
4 Sleeve pockets for awl, shears, and cutters

5 Large compartment for bulky tools, parts, and materials
6 Webbing handles with stitched grips
7 Carrying sling

Figure 2. Tentage repair kit case and carrying sling.

j. Bent Trimmer's Shears. The steel trimmer's shears (11) are about 10 inches long. They are used to trim damaged fabric, to cut thread, and to cut patches.

k. Sailmaker's Needles. The steel sailmaker's needles (12) have a triangular section with rounded edges that taper to a sharp point at one end and round off to the eye at the other. The kit has 25 size 14 needles, the size most used to sew canvas.

l. Tent Line Slips. Tent line slips (13) are used to adjust the length of tent lines. A slip is a 4-inch-long magnesium casting that is shaped like a barbell. In each end of the slip is a 7/16-inch hole through which tent lines can be run to adjust slack.

m. Carrying Sling. The carrying sling (14, fig 1 and 7, fig 2) is a standard, general-purpose strap, made of medium-weight webbing. It has a 1-inch snaphook at each end. The snaphooks are used to attach the sling to D-rings at the top of the case. To prevent loss, the sling is generally left attached to the case.

n. Sewing Palm. The sewing palm (15) is a leather shield worn over the palm of the hand to protect the hand from the needle and to help push the needle through the material. The sewing palm has a metal inset with small dents to hold the end of the needle while it is being forced through tent material.

o. Slide-Fastener Lubricant. The kit has a box of 24 sticks of interlocking-slide-fastener lubri-cant (16). The lubricant is applied by rubbing the lubricant stick up and down the slide fastener.

p. Punch-and-Die Sets. Punch-and-die (17) sets are used to insert grommets in tents. The kit has two sets, one for the No. 4 grommets and one for the No. 5 grommets. The sets are used to clinch together the halves of each grommet.

q. Saddler's Sewing Awl. The saddler's sewing awl (18) is used for lockstitching by hand. Two straight needles and one needle curved at the point come with the awl. The straight needles are used where there is room to manipulate the awl needle from a reel or bobbin set in close quarters, such as inside corners. The thread or cord is fed to the awl needle from a reel or bobbin set in the handle. The needle is secured to the awl handle with a two-jaw chuck.

r. Round Connecting Rings. The kit has three sizes of connecting rings (19), 1/2-inch diameter, 3/4-inch diameter, and 1-inch diameter. The rings are used to reinforce grommet holes.

s. Cloth. Cotton duck cloth (20) weighing about 9.85 ounces per square yard is furnished in 8-yard bolts. The olive-drab duck is resistant to fire, water, mildew, and weather. It is used to patch tents.

t. Other Data.

(1) *Dimensions.* The overall dimensions of the tentage repair kit, complete with tools, parts, and materials, are 16 by 16 by 12 inches.

Table 1. Repair Kit, Tentage,

No. per kit	Unit	Nomenclature
6	cn	Adhesive.
1	ea	Awl, saddler's sewing, with needles.
1	ck	Beeswax, technical.
1	ea	Brush, wire, scratch.
1	ea	Case, tentage, repair kit.
8	yd	Cloth, duck cotton.
1	gr	Grommet, metallic, 0.320-in. height of barrel, size No. 4.
1	hd	Grommet, metallic, 0.380-in. height of barrel, size No. 5.
1	box	Lubricant, interlocking slide fastener.
1	ea	Mallet, rawhide.
1	pkg	Needle, sailmaker's size 14.
1	ea	Palm, sewing
1	ea	Punch, cutting, double bow, 1/2-in. diameter of hole, size No. 5.
1	ea	Punch, cutting, double bow, 9/16-in. diameter of hole, size No. 6.
50	ea	Rig, connecting, round, 1/2-in. inside diameter.
25	ea	Ring, connecting, round, 3/4-in. inside diameter.
10	ea	Ring, connecting, round, 1-in. inside diameter.
1	ea	Set, punch and dies, grommet isserting, size No. 4.
1	ea	Set, punch and die, grommet inserting, size No. 5.
1	ea	Shears, bent, trimmer's.
1	ea	Sling, carrying bag and case.
10	ea	Slip, tent line.
1	tube	Thread, polyester.
1	pound	Twine.
1	ea	TM 10–269.

(2) *Weight.* The weight of the tentage repair kit, complete with tools, parts, and materials, is approximately 30 1/2 pounds.

(3) *Carrying sling.* The carrying sling of the kit has a minimum adjustment of 28 1/2-inches and a maximum adjustment of 48 inches.

(4) *Tools, parts, and materials.* Tabulated information on the tools, parts, and materials of the tentage repair kit is contained in table 1.

6. Marking Areas for Repair

Canvas and webbing items are inspected for weakened areas, holes, tears, opened seams, and missing parts such as hardware and lines. When fabric damage or missing parts are noted, the inspecting repairman marks with chalk the area for repair or the part to be replaced. Seven different markings (fig 3) are used to indicate the types of repair.

a. Circle. A circle (A) indicates:

(1) On items other than tents that minor repairs such as darning or tacking are needed.

(2) On tents that a hole or tear is under 4 3/4 inches in diameter or length and is to be repaired by a cement patch.

Note. If a sewing machine is available, a machine-sewn patch should always be used.

b. Rectangle. A rectangle (B) indicates:

(1) On items other than tents that a machine-sewn patch is required.

(2) On tents, that the damaged area is greater than 4 3/4 inches in diameter or length and requires a machine- or hand-sewn patch. If the damaged area, regardless of size, supports hardware and is subject to strain, it must be repaired by a sewn patch.

c. Arrow. An arrow (C) indicates:

(1) Hidden damage.

(2) Missing hardware.

d. Parallel Lines. Parallel lines (D) indicate an open seam. A line is chalked along each side of the open seam, parallel to the seam and extending the distance to be sewn.

e. Cross. A cross (E) indicates:

(1) A damaged or missing part is on the inside.

(2) An old patch must be replaced.

(3) A section or panel must be replaced.

f. WP. The symbol "WP" (F) indicates that waterproofing is required. It is marked on the doors.

g. Mildew. The symbol "MILDEW" (G) with a circle around it is marked in an area to indicate that mildew is present.

7. Hand Sewing

For many repairs, canvas and webbing must be sewn by hand. Hand sewing is necessary when sewing machines are not available, when it is impractical to use a machine because of the size of the article to be repaired, or when the damaged area cannot be conveniently placed under the machine needle. The simplest of the hand-stitches may be used to make repairs to canvas. Only a needle, palm, thread, beeswax, and canvas are needed. Before any hand-sewn repairs are attempted, instructions should be carefully studied.

a. Handstitches. Repairmen commonly use the following stitches (fig 4) for hand sewing canvas:

(1) *Flat stitch (A).* Pass the needle over and under an equal amount of material, each successive stitch entering the material from the opposite side. This stitch is used as a temporary fastening until machine repairs can be made.

(2) *Round stitch (B).* Insert the needle at right angles to the edge of the material, and bring the cord around the edge before making the next stitch. The round stitch is used to handwork grommets.

(3) *Overcast stitch (C).* Insert the needle through the material at an angle so that it comes out to one side and ahead of the point of insertion, and bring the cord over to the original line of insertion before making the next stitch. This stitch is used to apply a hand-sewn patch.

(4) *Backstitch (D).* The backstitch is so named because the needle is always set back half a stitch length into the last stitch made. Make two small stitches in the same place to secure the end of the cord. Then continue by inserting the needle into the middle of the preceding stitch and bringing it out on the same side of the material a stitch length in advance of the last stitch. The backstitch is used to secure an open seam.

(5) *Fishbone stitch (E).* The fishbone stitch, similar to the baseball stitch, is used to join the edges of a tear until a hand-sewn or cement patch is applied. Insert the needle through between the two edges to be sewn together. Then take a diagonal stitch from one side toward the other, bringing the needle out between the two edges. Repeat this operation on the other side of the tear, and continue the stitching, alternating from side to side. To keep the stitches uniform, hold the edges smoothly together. Make the stitches firmly, but do not pull them tight enough to pucker the fabric.

b. Beginning and Finishing a Line of Handstitching.

(1) *Beginning.* To begin a line of handstitching, use one of the following methods:

(a) Put the needle in the right side and take a short stitch. Draw the needle through

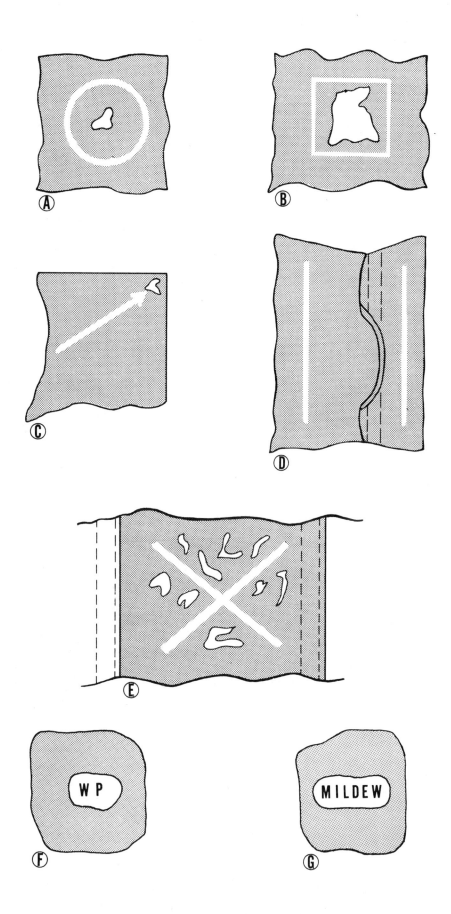

Figure 3. Markings used to indicate types of repair.

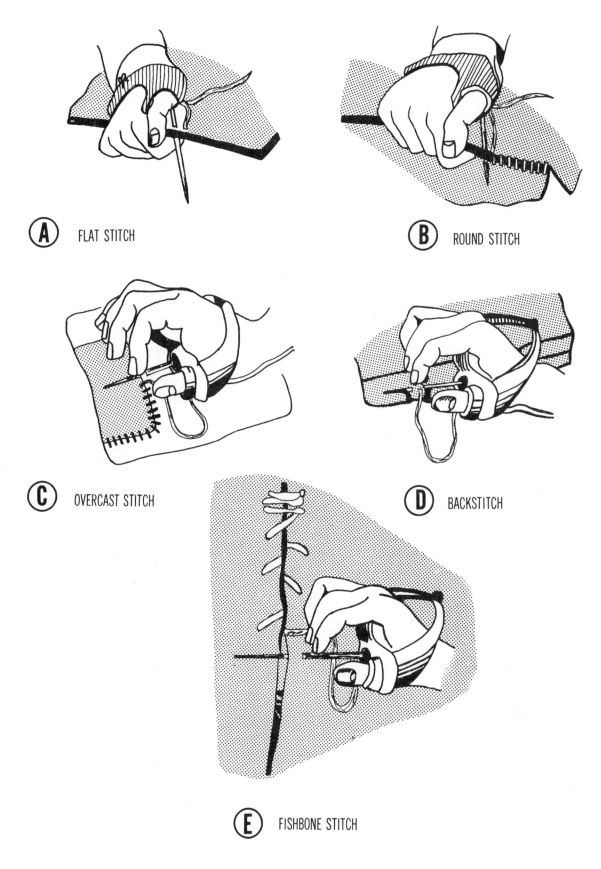

A FLAT STITCH

B ROUND STITCH

C OVERCAST STITCH

D BACKSTITCH

E FISHBONE STITCH

Figure 4. Common stitches used in hand sewing.

until only a small end shows. Take a stitch or two back over the stitch just made to fasten the thread end securely.

(b) Put the needle through the canvas so that the end of the thread stays on the unfinished side. Draw the thread through until a 1/2-inch to 1-inch end shows. Lay the thread end along the line of stitching so that the succeeding stitches cover the end and lock it in place.

(2) *Finishing.* To finish a line of hand-stitching, use one of the following methods:

(a) Make one or two stitches back over the last stitch made, and bring the needle to the underside. Hold the thread down to the fabric with the left thumb, and pass the needle under the thread. Draw the thread up tight, and make a knot, still holding the thread close to the fabric with the thumb. Repeat this operation for a stronger knot, and then clip the thread.

(b) Reverse the direction of the needle, and thrust it back under the final two stitches. Draw the thread tight, and clip it.

c. *Using the Sewing Palm.* Place the sewing palm (fig 5) over the hand so that the leather strap is around the hand, with the thumb through the thumb opening and the palm part against the palm of the hand. See that the metal seat of the palm is at the base of the thumb, with the pelletlike depression facing the fingers. Use the metal seat of the palm to push the sail-maker's needle entirely through the fabric.

d. *Preparing Needle and Thread.* To prepare the needle and thread for sewing, proceed as follows:

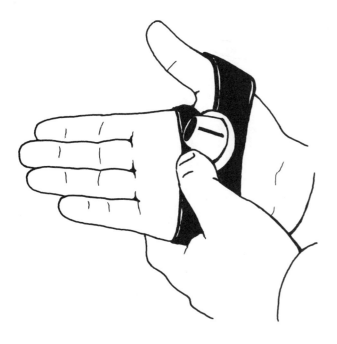

Figure 5. Sewing palm.

(1) *Waxing thread.* Before putting the thread through the needle, wax it by drawing it across the cake of beeswax (fig 6) provided for this purpose. Wax twice the length of two-strand thread and four times the length of four-strand thread.

(2) *Threading needle.* To thread the needle, make a bend or loop in the thread and push the loop through the eye of the needle (fig 7). To make a double-strand thread, make the loop near one end of the piece of thread, and pull the single strand through the eye of the needle to a point midway between the free ends. To make a four-strand thread, form the loop midway between the free ends, and pull the double strands midway between the two free ends (fig 8).

(3) *Rewaxing thread.* Twist the strands together, and give the twisted thread a thorough waxing (fig 9).

(4) *Securing thread ends.* Secure the free ends of the loop end of the thread with a knot.

8. Hand Sewing with Saddler's Sewing Awl

To handstitch extra-heavy canvas or several thicknesses of canvas, use the saddler's sewing awl, the only tool needed. Before making any lockstitch repairs, study the instructions and illustrations.

a. *Threading the Awl.* To thread the saddler's sewing awl (fig 10), proceed as follows:

(1) Remove the bobbin cap (1), and withdraw the bobbin (2) from the bobbin chamber.

(2) Pass the end of the bobbin thread into the bobbin chamber and out through the small hole in the side of the handle (3).

(3) Replace the bobbin and the bobbin cap.

(4) Pass the thread along the outside of the awl handle, and make one turn around the tension post (4).

Note. When passing the thread around the tension post, pass it under the thread running from the bobbin chamber to the post. If passed over the thread, it will not feed freely.

(5) Remove the chuck cap (7), and pass the thread down through the slot under the ferrule (5) and along the groove between the chuck jaws (6).

(6) Place the needle in the chuck with the long needle groove in line with the groove between the chuck jaws.

(7) Replace the chuck cap, and screw it down as tight as possible to hold the needle in the chuck.

(8) Run one-half of an inch of thread through the eye of the needle (8). Bend the half-inch end back so it will lie along the short groove side of the needle. The awl is now ready for making the lockstitch.

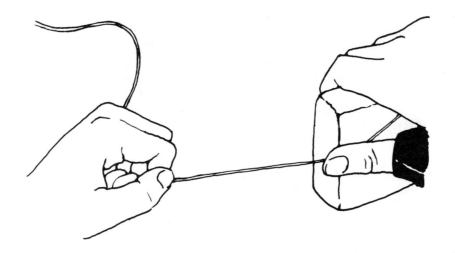

Figure 6. Waxing thread.

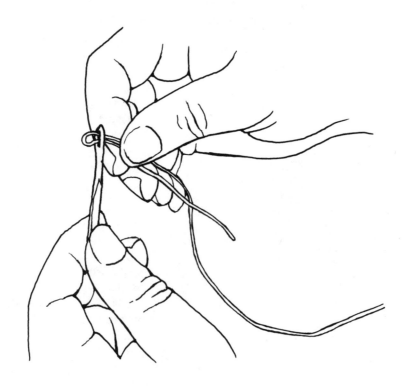

Figure 7. Threading needle.

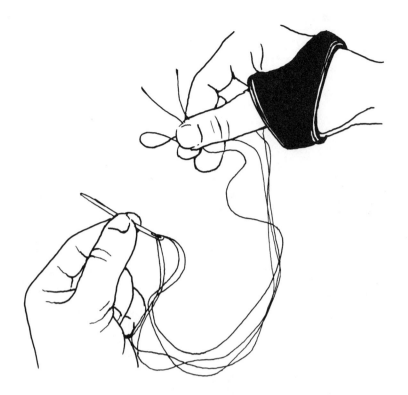

Figure 8. Making a four-strand thread.

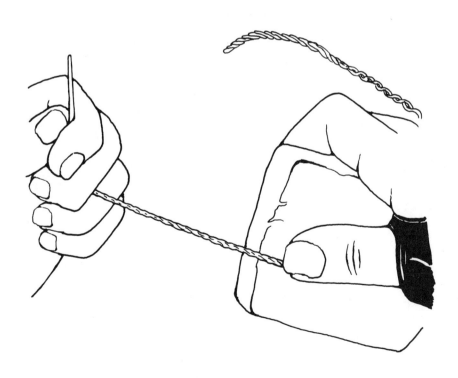

Figure 9. Rewaxing a twisted thread.

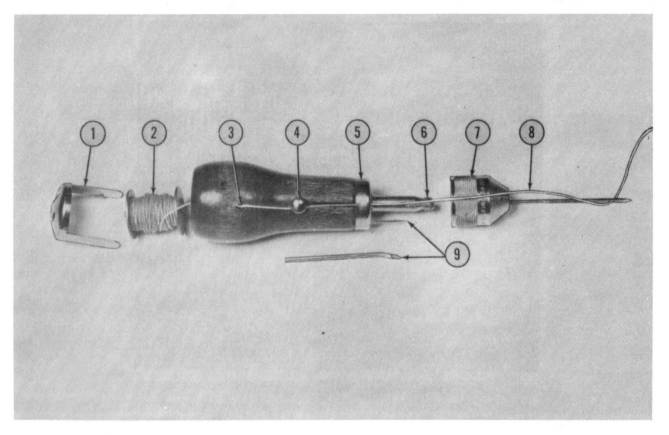

1	Bobbin cap	6	Groove between chuck jaws
2	Bobbin	7	Chuck cap
3	Hole for bobbin thread	8	Needle
4	Tension post	9	Additional needles
5	Ferrule		

Figure 10. Threaded saddler's sewing awl.

*b. Making the Lockstitch. T*o make a line of lockstitching with the saddler's awl, proceed as follows:

(1) See that the awl needle is threaded and that not more than half an inch of thread extends through the eye of the needle. See also that the thread lies along the groove between the chuck jaws in line with the long groove of the needle.

(2) Grasp the thread just below the tension post, and pull out some slack from the bobbin. Since this slack provides the bottom thread for the lockstitch, withdraw ample thread to reach from the start to the finish of the proposed line of stitching (fig 11).

(3) Thrust the awl needle through the material far enough to carry through the half-inch thread end. Then, with the needle still inserted, grasp the half-inch end, and pull it until all the slack thread is on the underside of the material (fig 12).

(4) Withdraw the needle, leaving the slack on the underside of the material.

(5) To make the first stitch, push the needle through the material again, a stitch length from

the first insertion, and this time draw the needle halfway back. Drawing back the needle causes the thread to form a loop on the underside of the material. With the left hand, pass the bottom thread through the loop (fig 13), and draw through all the slack thread.

(6) Withdraw the needle allowing the needle thread to loop around the bottom thread (fig 14).

(7) Pull the needle through while holding the bottom thread, and pull until the stitch is tight (fig 15).

(8) Continue the line of stitching, repeating the operation in (5) through (7) above.

(9) Finish the stitching by thrusting the needle through the material and then withdrawing it halfway. Cut the loop thus formed, withdraw the needle, and secure the two loose ends on the underside of the material with a square knot (fig 16).

Note. The proper tension on both the needle thread and the bottom thread results in a perfect stitch locked in the center of the material (A, fig 17). Pulling too hard on the needle thread causes the stitch to lock on top of the material (B), whereas not pulling hard enough lets the stitch lock on the underside of the material (C).

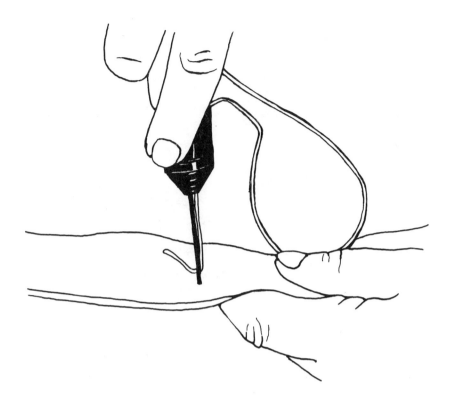

Figure 11. Saddler's sewing awl, showing bobbin thread
pulled slack and ready for sewing.

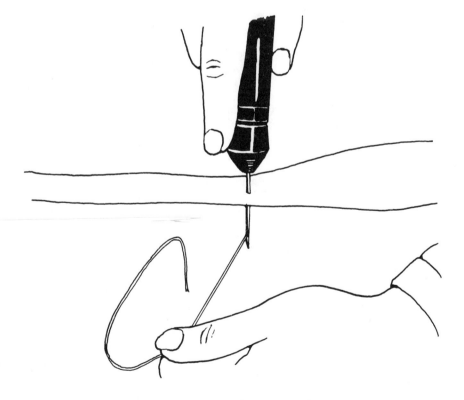

Figure 12. Saddler's sewing awl, showing slack thread
pulled through the material to form bottom thread.

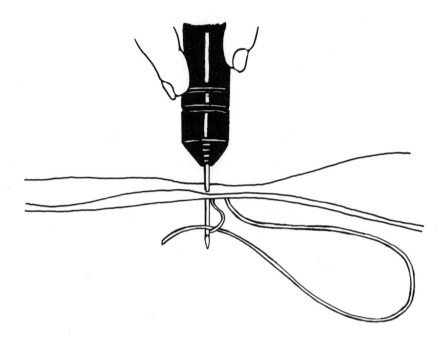

*Figure 13.   Saddler's sewing awl, withdrawn halfway,
showing the loop thus formed and the bottom thread
being inserted through the loop.*

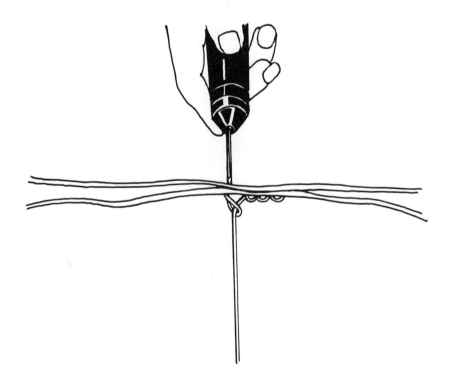

*Figure 14.   Saddler's sewing awl, showing the needle
thread looped to bottom thread.*

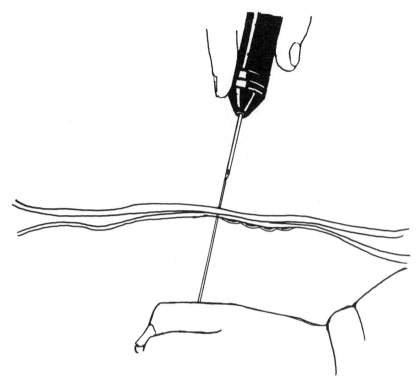

Figure 15.   Saddler's sewing awl, showing the stitch being drawn tight.

9. Machine Sewing

The machine sewing of canvas and webbing in the Army is normally done on a single-needle, lockstitch machine with compound feed and high-lift alternating pressure. The machine is designed especially for the repair of canvas equipment and tents. In some instances, chainstitch machines are used.

a. Machine Sewing of Canvas.

(1) *Type of stitch.* When repairing canvas equipment and tents by machine, follow as nearly as possible the type of stitch used in the original construction of the item being repaired. The lockstitch, chainstitch, and bar tack are the stitches commonly used in the machine sewing of canvas and webbing.

(2) *Size of needle.* The size of the needle to be used is determined by the size of the thread. The machine will not stitch well if the thread does not pass freely through the eye of the needle. Size 24 sewing-machine needles are commonly used in the repair of heavy canvas, and size 22 in the repair of lightweight canvas.

(3) *Thread.* Type I or type II, class I polyester thread is generally used for machine sewing. Left-twist thread is used for the needle, and either left- or right-twist thread for the bobbin. Thread size FF is commonly used in the repair

of heavy canvas, and sizes F and E in the repair of lightweight canvas.

(4) *Thread tension.* Adjust the tension of the needle and bobbin threads so that the threads lock in the center of the thickness of the material (A, fig 17). If the tension of the needle thread is greater than that of the bobbin thread, a faulty stitch will result, with the needle thread lying straight along the upper side of the material (B). If the bobbin thread is tighter than the needle thread, a poorly made stitch will result, with the bobbin thread lying along the underside of the material (C).

(5) *Length of stitch.* The length of the stitch is determined by the number of stitches per inch (the longer the stitch, the fewer stitches per inch).

b. Seams. The seams (fig 18) commonly used in canvas repair are as follows:

(1) *Simple seam.* The simple seam (A) consists of a series of stitches that joins two or more pieces of material. Generally, this seam is used to join pieces of material that do not require a finished seam edge. To make the simple seam, refer to A, figure 18 and proceed as follows:

(*a*) Place the faces of two pieces of material together, with the edges even.

(*b*) To join the two pieces, sew a straight row of stitches parallel to the edge of the material and one-fourth inch from the edge.

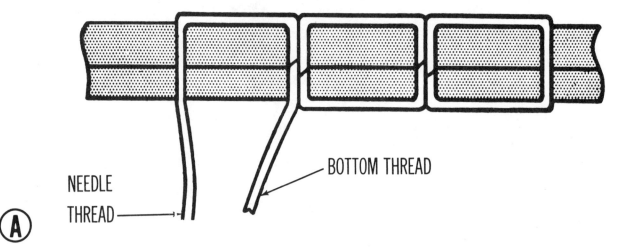

NEEDLE THREAD →

BOTTOM THREAD →

Ⓐ

VIEW SHOWING LOOSE THREAD ENDS REMAINING AFTER
NEEDLE THREAD HAS BEEN CUT AND NEEDLE WITHDRAWN

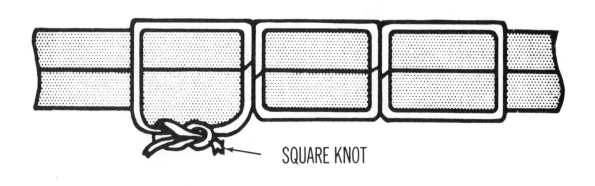

SQUARE KNOT →

Ⓑ

VIEW SHOWING FREE ENDS SECURED WITH A SQUARE KNOT

*Figure 16. Cross-section views of lockstitching showing
methods of finishing a line.*

(*c*) Tack the seam no more than 1 inch
and no less than three-fourths inch at the beginning and at the end of the seam. Tack stitches
should be in the same row used to join the two
pieces of material.

Note. For lightweight materials, such as burlap, the
stitch row should be no closer than 1 inch from the edge
of the materials. If the stitch row is any closer, lightweight materials may pull apart.

(2) *Flat seam.* The flat seam (B) is used
to join two or more pieces of material when the
seam has to be finished outside and inside, such
as seams of tents, paulins, and truck covers. The

materials joined must have selvage edges. To
make the flat seam, refer to B, figure 18, and
proceed as follows:

(*a*) Place one piece of material face up
on a table, with the selvage edge to the left.
With chalk, mark a straight line parallel with
the selvage edge and 1 inch from the edge.

(*b*) Place the second piece of material
face up on the first piece so that the selvage
edge lines up with the chalk line.

(*c*) Sew a straight row of stitches one-
eighth inch from the selvage edge.

(*d*) Tack each end of the stitch row.

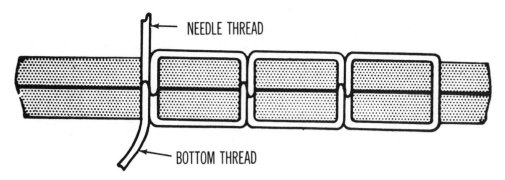

NEEDLE THREAD

BOTTOM THREAD

(A) PERFECT LOCKSTITCH WITH NEEDLE THREAD AND BOTTOM THREAD LOCKED IN CENTER OF THE MATERIAL

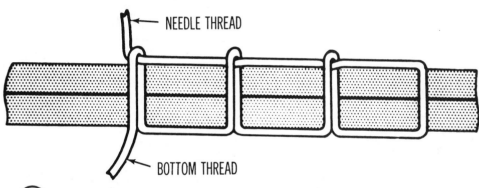

NEEDLE THREAD

BOTTOM THREAD

(B) FAULTY LOCKSTITCH WITH NEEDLE THREAD PULLED TOO FAR, BRINGING BOTTOM THREAD TO TOP OF MATERIAL

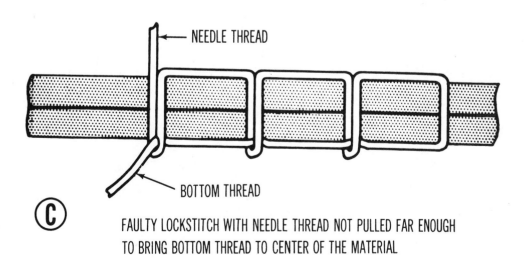

NEEDLE THREAD

BOTTOM THREAD

(C) FAULTY LOCKSTITCH WITH NEEDLE THREAD NOT PULLED FAR ENOUGH TO BRING BOTTOM THREAD TO CENTER OF THE MATERIAL

Figure 17. Perfect and faulty lockstitches.

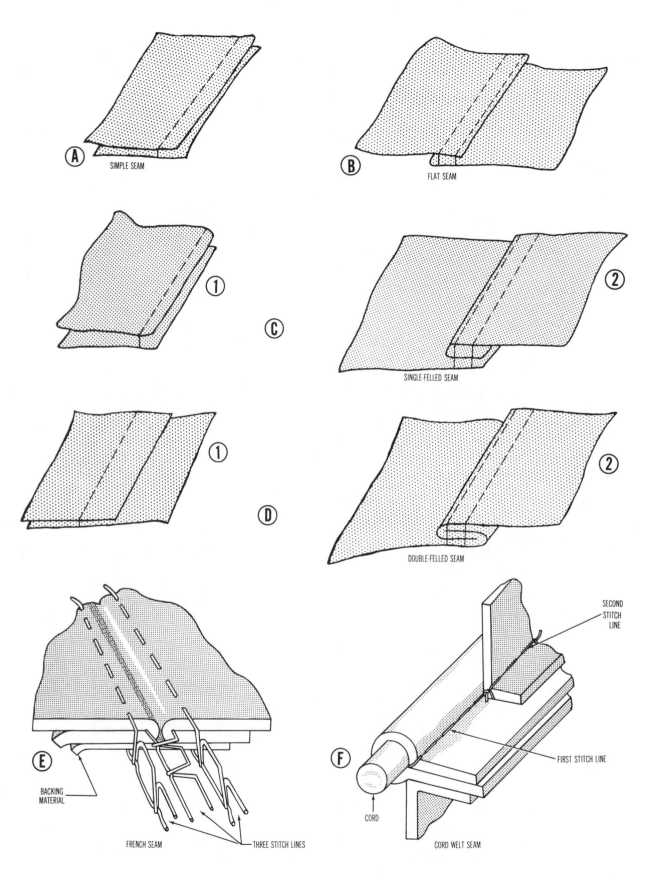

A — SIMPLE SEAM

B — FLAT SEAM

C — ① ②

SINGLE-FELLED SEAM

D — ① ②

DOUBLE-FELLED SEAM

E — FRENCH SEAM

BACKING MATERIAL

THREE STITCH LINES

F — CORD WELT SEAM

SECOND STITCH LINE

FIRST STITCH LINE

CORD

Figure 18.   Seams commonly used in canvas repair.

(e) Turn both pieces of material over, and stitch a second row of stitches one-eighth inch from the selvage edge of the second piece.

(f) Tack each end of the stitch row.

(3) *Single-felled seam.* The single-felled seam (C) like the simple and flat seam, is used to join two or more pieces of material. It is used to join materials when the top side, or outside, of the seam should be finished but the underside may have raw edges. The single-felled seam is also used to sew on patches. The materials to be joined may have raw edges. To make the single-felled seam, refer to C, figure 18 and proceed as follows:

(a) Sew two pieces of material together with a simple seam as described in (1) above, except that the stitch row should be 1 inch from the edge of the material (C1).

(b) Fold the top piece of material to the right, and sew a row of stitches one-eighth inch from the fold (C2). Tack each end of the stitch row.

(c) Turn both pieces of material over, and sew a row of stitches one-eighth inch from the raw edges of the material. Tack each end of the stitch row.

(4) *Double-felled seam.* The double-felled seam (D) is used to join two pieces of material when both the top side and underside of the seam should be finished, without exposed raw edges. To make the double-felled seam, refer to D, figure 18, and proceed as follows:

(a) Place one piece of the material face up on the table, and mark with chalk a straight line parallel to the right edge and 1 inch from the edge.

(b) Place the second piece of material face down on the table, and mark with chalk a straight line parallel to the right edge and 1 inch from the edge.

(c) Place the second piece of material face down on the first piece so that the chalkline faces up. (The two pieces of material should be face to face.) Aline the right edge of the second piece of material with the chalkline on the first piece.

(d) Join the two pieces of material by sewing a straight row of stitches on the chalkline of the top piece of material (D1). Tack each end of the stitch row. .

(e) Fold the right edge of the bottom piece of material to the left, and fold the left edge of the top piece of material to the right.

(f) Sew two rows of stitches, each row one-eighth inch from a folded edge (D2). Tack each end of each stitch row.

(5) *French seam.* The french seam (E) is used mostly for tops and seats. Make a plain seam first, then fold the edges back away from the seam and add the two additional rows of stitching, sewing the joined pieces to a piece of backing material.

(6) *Cord welt seam.* The cord welt seam (F) used particularly in seat covers, is made by doubling a piece of material around a cord and fastening it with a plain seam. The strip thus formed is then sewed between the two pieces to be joined.

10. Edge Bindings

A binding made from a narrow strip of material or tape is used to strengthen edges of material (fig 19). When a binding attachment is not available, stitch the binding first to the inside of the material, and then fold the binding over to the outside and stitch it in place (A). Figure 19 (B) and (C) shows alternative methods of binding mats or carpets. To use these methods proceed as follows:

a. Roll Stitch Mat Binding. To make this binding (B), make a plain seam first by sewing the binding to the mat or carpet. Then roll the binding around underneath the mat and stitch a second row along the turn-over edge of the binding. If the material is carpet, these stitches will disappear in the nap; thus all sewing in the seam will be invisible.

b. Plain Mat Binding. To make this binding (C), fold one edge of the binding to the inside of the mat. Then fold the binding underneath the mat and apply a single line of stitches.

11. Darning

Small holes and worn areas, except in tents, may be repaired by either hand or machine darning. Common types of darns (fig 20) are used as follows:

a. A circular darn (A), starting at the outside of the damaged area and ending at the center, is used for small holes and worn areas under one-half of an inch in diameter.

b. An up-and-down, or zigzag, darn (B) is used for slits or straight tears.

c. An overedge darn (C) is used when wear occurs on corded seams or bindings.

d. A darn with reinforcement (D) is used for holes one-fourth to three-fourths of an inch in diameter. A reinforcing piece is placed underneath the hole before the hole is darned.

12. Hemming

Exposed or raw edges of material should be turned under and stitched down to prevent raveling of the material and to give the material a finished appearance. This procedure is called

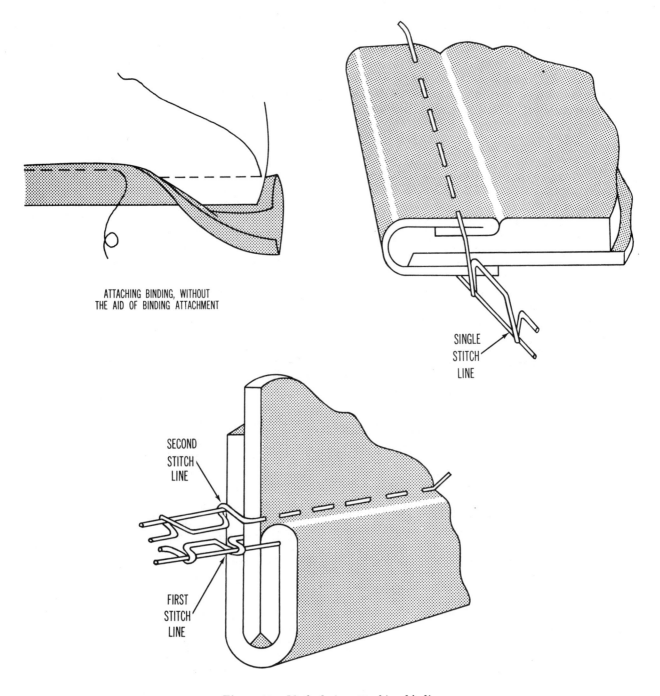

ATTACHING BINDING, WITHOUT
THE AID OF BINDING ATTACHMENT

SINGLE
STITCH
LINE

SECOND
STITCH
LINE

FIRST
STITCH
LINE

Figure 19. Methods for attaching binding.

hemming. Hems can be made in various widths, depending on the use of the item being fabricated or repaired. Common types of hems are described below.

a. A hem used to finish the edge of an item, without the use of grommets, is made by allowing 1 inch of material for the hem and one-half of an inch for the felling or turnunder. The hem is sewed one-eighth of an inch from the folded edge of the turnunder, and each end of the stitch row is tacked at least 1 inch.

b. A hem that is to have grommets installed in it is made by allowing at least 2 inches of material for the hem and 2 inches for the turnunder. The hem is sewed as in *a* above.

c. A hem made completely around a piece of material requires that the material be folded in a way that the corners can be stitched properly. This type of hem, if made for grommets to be installed, is made with the hem and turnunder widths the same as in *b* above, or if made just for turning under the raw edges for finishing, the same as in *a* above. This type of hem (fig 21) is made as follows:

(1) Make the hem as in *a* or *b* above, but stop the stitch line 2½ inches before reaching the next edge (1), and do not backstitch.

(2) Fold the second edge inward (2).

(3) Fold the second edge under, hiding the raw edge (3). Sew onto the second folded edge one stitch length. Turn the material, and sew diagonally to the outside corner. Turn the ma-

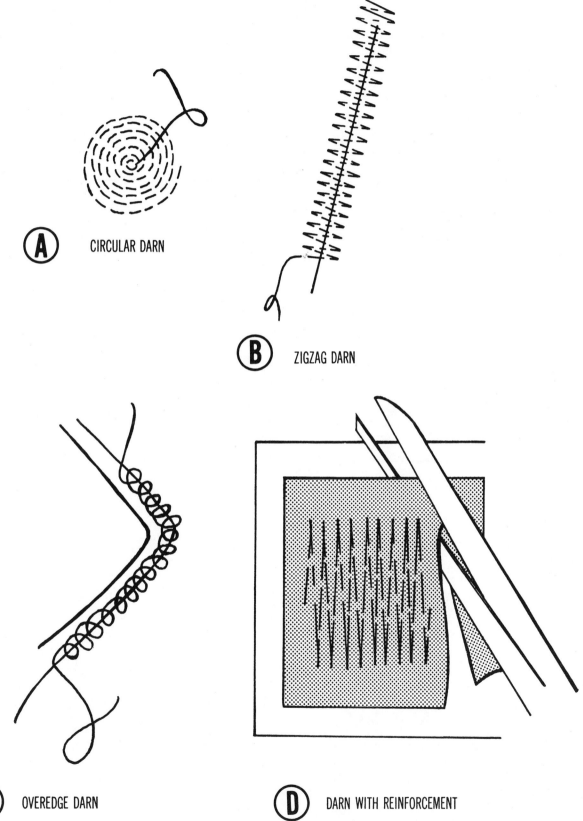

(A) CIRCULAR DARN

(B) ZIGZAG DARN

(C) OVEREDGE DARN

(D) DARN WITH REINFORCEMENT

Figure 20. Common types of darns.

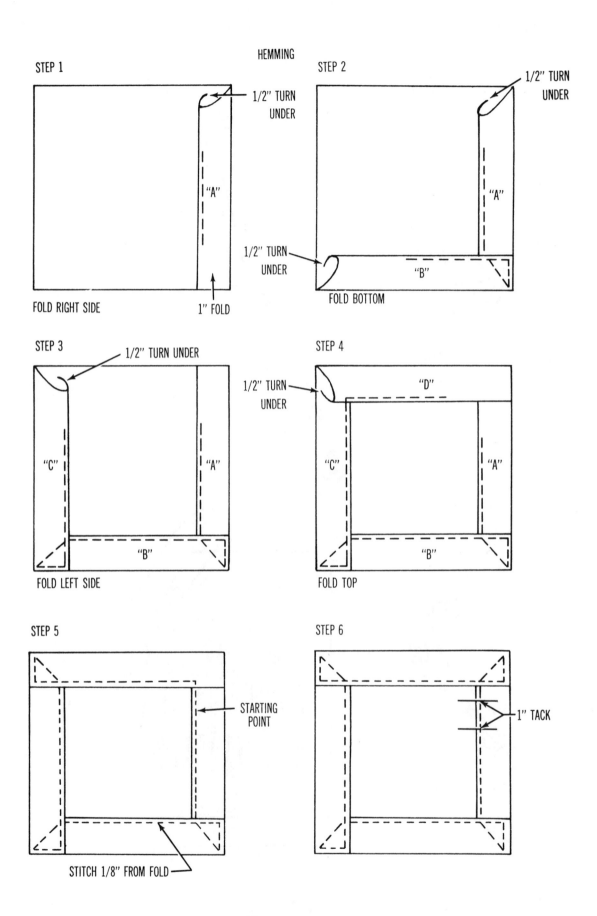

Figure 21. Hemming.

terial, and sew across the end of the second folded edge. Now turn the material, and stitch along the second folded edge, stopping 2½ inches from third edge.

(4) Continue this procedure until all four edges and corners are sewn (5), and backstitch the last corner at least 1 inch (6).

13. Patching

Holes or tears in canvas equipment that are over one-eighth of an inch in diameter or length require patching. Damaged tent tops require patching on all holes and tears. Items made of waterproof, fire-resistant, and mildew-resistant fabric must be patched with similarly treated material. The material used for patching should match the color and texture of the item. The following patches are customarily used in the repair of canvas and webbing items:

a. Top Patches. Top patches are applied to the top side of the material. A top patch may be a simple patch or a felled patch.

(1) *Simple top patch.* Make a simple top patch (fig 22) as follows:

(*a*) If practical, zigzag stitch the torn edges together (A).

(*b*) Center the patch over the damaged area, allowing a minimum overlap of 2 inches on all sides (plus three-fourths inch for turn under of all edges.)

(*c*) Turn under the edges of the patch three-fourths of an inch, and sew the patch in place, taking care to keep one edge of the patch parallel with one edge of the item being repaired and the stitching not more than one-eighth of an inch from the edges of the patch. For tents, sew two rows of stitching (D) before cutting away the damaged area. A distance of three-eighths to one-half of an inch between stitch rows is adequate. Tack each stitch row by sewing at least 1 inch over the starting point.

(*d*) Unless the hole has been zigzag stitched ((*a*) above), cut away the damaged area (B through D).

(2) *Felled top patch.* The felled top patch (fig 23) differs from the simple top patch only in the manner of finishing. After stitching the patch in place from the top side, turn the material over, cut away the damaged area, notch the corners, turn the edges in (A), and stitch the turned edges to the patch. Turn the material top side up (B).

b. Inverted Patch. An inverted patch (fig 24) is one that is placed on the underside of the material. An inverted patch, either simple or felled, is stitched and finished in the same manner as the top patch, but care must be taken to center the inverted patch *under* the damaged area.

c. Strap-Support Patches. Strap-support patches are used to repair damaged strap-support areas. The patches may be of single thickness where the strain is slight, or of double thickness where increased tensile strength is required.

(1) *Single-thickness patch.* This patch is a felled top patch. It may be made from a salvaged piece of material with the strap attached. Figure 25 shows an inside view of a single-thickness strap-support patch.

(2) *Double-thickness patch.* The double-thickness patch (fig 26) is a two-patch combination using both the inverted patch and the top patch. Make the double-thickness patch as follows:

(*a*) Cut two patches large enough to cover the damaged area. Allow a 2-inch margin plus three-fourths inch for turnunder on all edges of each patch.

(*b*) Turn the item wrong side up, and center the inverted patch over the damaged area (A).

(*c*) Turn under the patch edges, and stitch the patch in place (A).

(*d*) Turn the item right side up, and cut away the damaged area.

(*e*) Center the top patch over the inverted patch (B).

(*f*) Turn under the patch edges so that the top patch and the inverted patch are the same size (B).

(*g*) Finish by stitching the top patch in place (B).

d. Grommet Patches. A grommet patch is used to replace a damaged grommet support area where a grommet has torn loose from the fabric. Grommet patches most commonly used in the repair of canvas and webbing are as follows:

(1) *Overedge grommet patch.* The overedge grommet patch (fig 27) is made by folding the patch material over the damaged grommet support area (A1). The damage is covered on both the top and the bottom. The patch is then stitched in place, and a new grommet is inserted (A2). If the fabric containing a row of grommets is damaged, the entire edge is cut away and replaced with a new edge and new grommets (B).

(2) *Reinforced grommet patch.* Corners containing grommets are subject to much strain. To replace a corner grommet, use a reinforced patch of three thicknesses of material (fig 28). Make the reinforced grommet patch as follows:

(*a*) Cut away the damaged corner (A).

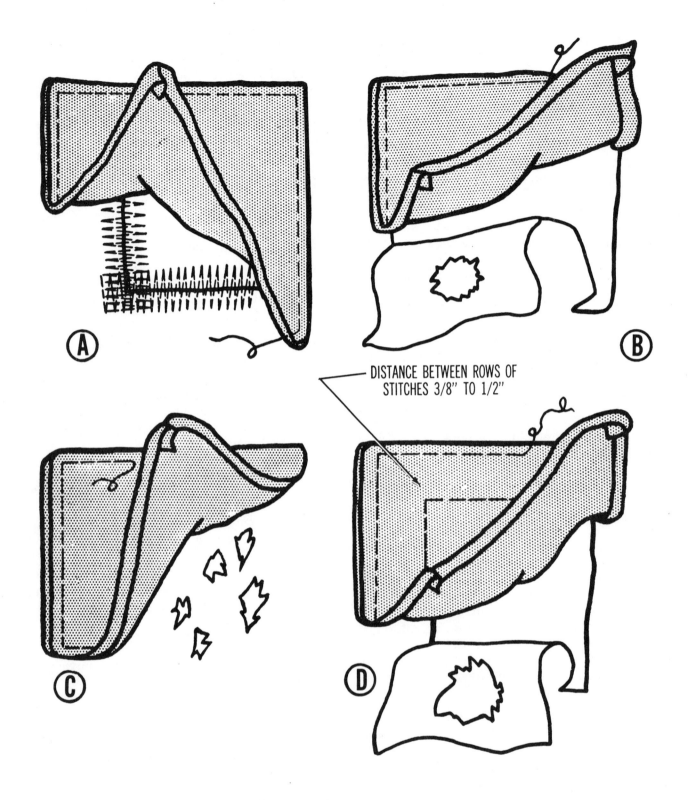

DISTANCE BETWEEN ROWS OF STITCHES 3/8" TO 1/2"

Figure 22. Simple top patches.

(*b*) Apply the patch to the underside, and stitch it in place.

(*c*) Apply the top patch, inserting an extra piece between the patches to give three thicknesses of material (B).

(*d*) Sew the top patch in place, and insert a new metal grommet (C).

(3) *Eave grommet patch.* When an eave grommet has torn loose or the fabric supporting an eave grommet is damaged, a four-ply patch (fig 29) is necessary to support the grommet

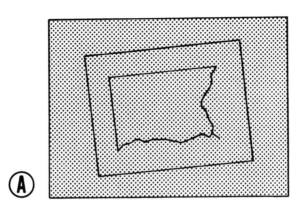

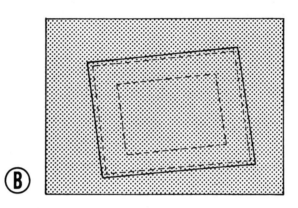

Figure 23. Felled top patch.

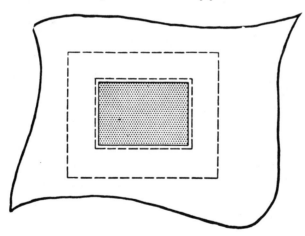

Figure 24. Inverted patch.

against the pull of the eaveline. Make the eave grommet patch as follows:

(a) Cut a patch large enough, when folded, to cover the damaged area with four thicknesses of material. The length of the patch material should be four times the width of the eave. The width of the patch should be sufficient to cover the damaged area and allow for an overlap of at least 2 inches on each side of the damage and a half-inch turnunder of the two edges.

(b) Fold in the side edges one-half of an inch (A).

(c) Fold each end of the patch toward the center so that they meet at the center of the patch (B).

(d) Fold the patch over the damaged eave so that two plies of material are on top of the eave and two are on the bottom (C).

(e) Sew the patch into place, and insert a new grommet (A2, fig 27).

e. Cement Patches. Tent holes or tears, depending on size and location, may be repaired with cement patches.

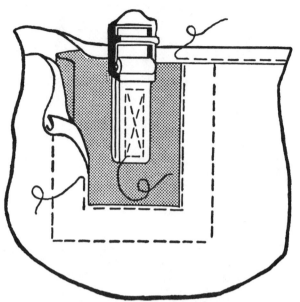

Figure 25. Single-thickness strap-support patch.

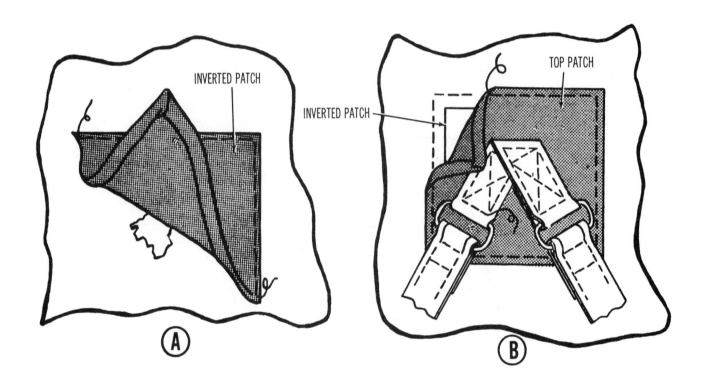

Figure 26. Double-thickness strap-support patch.

(1) *Large holes.* Round cement patches are used for patching tent holes no smaller than one-eighth of an inch nor larger than 4¾ inches in diameter or length, provided the holes are not on seams, edges, or areas supporting hardware. The materials needed for making a round cement patch are tent-patching cement (adhesive), a round cotton duck patch, a wire brush, a flat board for placing under the damaged area, and a paddle or stick for spreading the cement. Make a round cement patch as follows:

(*a*) Place a board under the damaged area to provide a flat working surface (fig 30).

(*b*) Clean the damaged area with the wire brush (fig 31).

(*c*) Measure the damaged area, and cut a patch that overlaps the damage with a margin

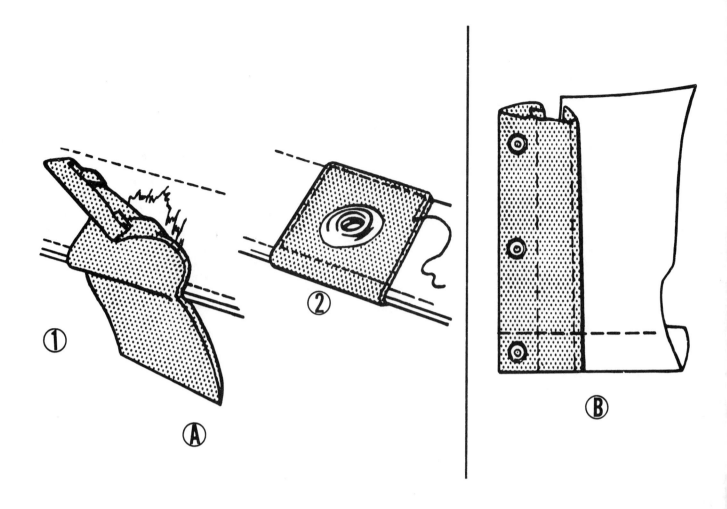

Figure 27. Overedge grommet patches.

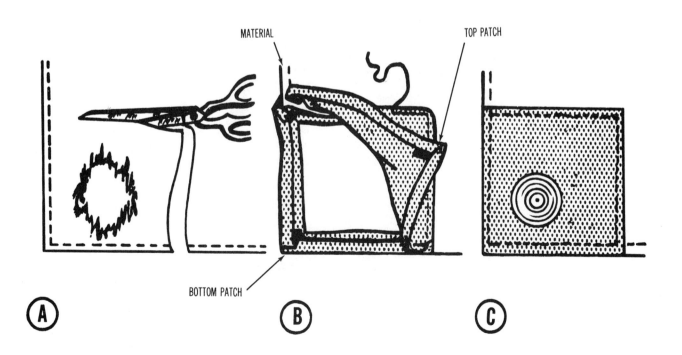

Figure 28. Reinforced grommet patch.

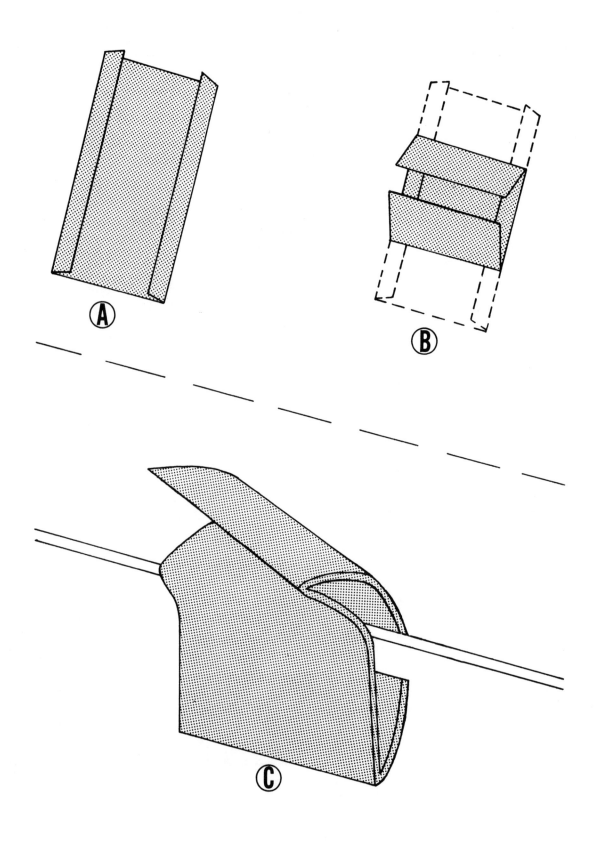

Figure 29. Eave grommet patch.

of at least three-fourths of an inch on all sides (fig 32).

(*d*) Center the patch over the damage, and while holding it in place, apply cement to the patch (fig 33).

(*e*) Apply cement over the edge of the patch to make a cement guide circle on the tent (fig 34).

(*f*) Lift the patch, and apply cement to the tent area inside the circle (fig 35).

(*g*) Allow the cement to dry, and apply a second coat.

(*h*) Press the cemented surfaces together while they are still tacky (fig 36).

(*i*) Roll any excess cement and air bubbles from under the patch, with a roller or ce-

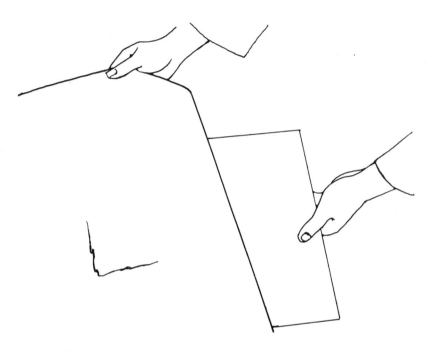

Figure 30. Placing board under damage, in preparation for round cement patch.

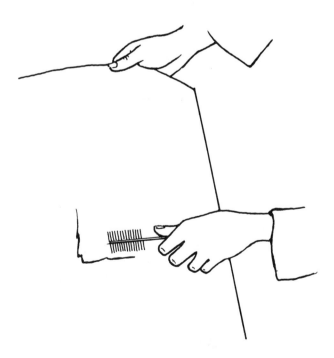

Figure 31. Cleaning tent canvas with wire brush, in preparation for round cement patch.

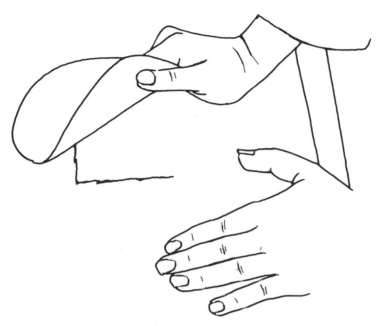

Figure 32.   Checking proper size of cement patch to cover damage.

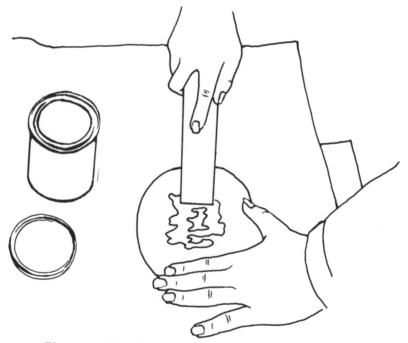

Figure 33.   Spreading cement on round cement patch.

ment can. This procedure insures proper bonding of the patch to the area.

(*j*) Seal the edge of the patch by applying cement with the tip of the finger (fig 37).

Note. For a pitched tent, a second repairman, working inside the tent, holds the board against the damaged area while the cement patch is being applied (fig 38).

(2) *Small holes.* A tent hole smaller than one-eighth of an inch (such as a spark hole) may be sealed with a dab of cement on the inside of the tent. Working on the inside surface of the tent, seal a small hole as follows:

(*a*) Clean the area around the hole to be sealed, preferably with a wire brush.

(*b*) Apply a dab of patching cement to the hole area. Using a stick or brush, work the cement into the fabric immediately surrounding the hole, and bridge the cement across the hole to seal it.

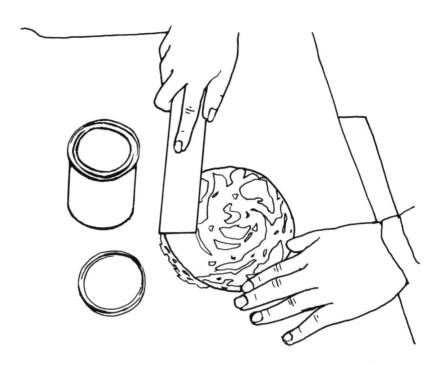

*Figure 34. Spreading cement over edge of round cement
patch to make marking on tent.*

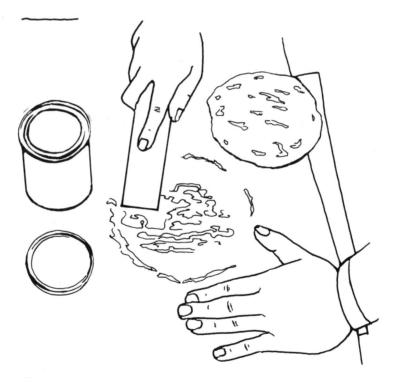

*Figure 35. Spreading cement on tent, in preparation for
round cement patch.*

f. Watershed Patch. The watershed patch (fig 39) is a top patch used on tentage. It differs from the rectangular top patch in that its top edge is angled to give a roof effect. The roof-type edge sheds water better than the straight, or flat-top, edge. Collecting less moisture in the top edge seaming, the watershed patch lasts longer than the rectangular patch. However, a rectangular patch may properly be placed directly under the eave of a tent where the top edge is protected or on the ridge of a tent where the patch straddles the ridge, leaving both top and bottom edges of the patch in a downward position. Make a watershed patch as follows:

(1) Select a piece of material of the same weight, color, treatment (fire- and mildew-resist-

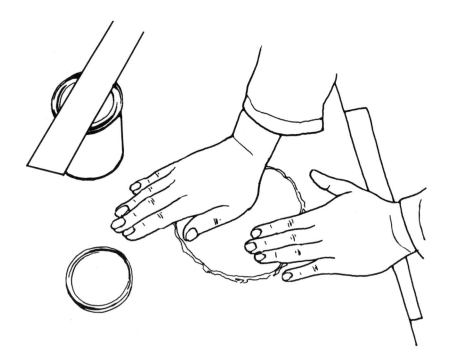

Figure 36. Pressing round cement patch over damaged area of tent.

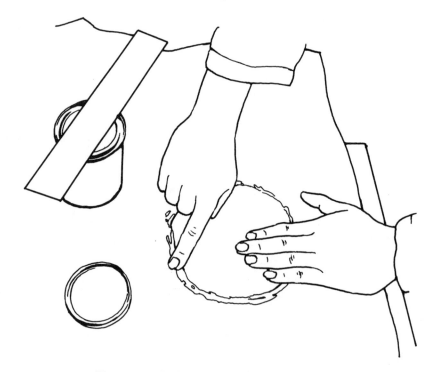

Figure 37. Sealing edge of round cement patch.

ant), and state of wear as that of the tent to be repaired.

(2) Cut a patch large enough to overlap 2 inches on all sides of the damaged area and to allow for three-fourths inch turnunder on each edge.

(3) Fold the patch in half lengthwise (A).

(4) On the folded patch, make a roof-type

top edge by cutting from the cut edges to the folded edge at a 22½° angle (B). (A 22½° angle can easily be made by first marking a 45° angle and then bisecting it.)

(5) Center the patch over the damaged area, turn under the patch edges, and stitch the patch in place with a row of stitches not more than one-eighth of an inch from the edge. (If

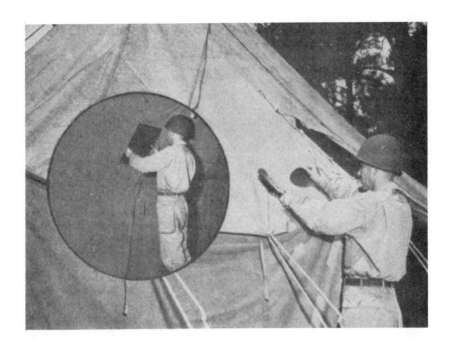

Figure 38. Applying cement patch to pitched tent, using two-man procedure.

the stitching is more than one-eighth of an inch from the edge, the seam collects water, shortening the life of the canvas.)

(6) Secure the patch to the tent with a second stitch row, placed three-eighths to one-half of an inch from the first row (C).

(7) Make sure both stitch rows are backstitched or tacked at least 1 inch to keep the stitches from pulling apart.

(8) Turn the tent over, and cut away the damaged material to within one-eighth of an inch of the inside stitch row.

Note. On tent side walls and on small tents, the watershed patch should be finished by felling (fig 23).

g. Patch Near Seam. When damage occurs near a seam (fig 40), repair it with either a rectangular or a watershed top patch, depending on the item to be repaired and the location of the damage to be covered. The construction of the patch to be used near a seam is similar to that of the top patches (*a* above) and that of the watershed patch (*f* above). The patch must be cut large enough to cover the damaged area and extend to the exposed edge of the seam. The patch, if on the top ply of the seam, is finished by two rows of stitches placed to match the original seam (A); if the patch is on the bottom ply of the seam, it is finished like a double-stitched top patch, with the seam edge tucked into the half-opened seam (B).

h. Overseam Patch. The overseam patch (fig 41) is used to repair a hole or a tear occurring on a seam (A). The overseam patch is in fact two half patches, one half applied to the top ply of the seam and the other half to the bottom ply (C). The patch may be either the rectangular or the watershed type, depending on its location. Make the watershed overseam patch as follows:

(1) Open the seam 6 inches above and below the damaged area (B).

(2) Cut a piece of patch material large enough to extend 2 inches on all sides of the damaged area, allowing for a ¾-inch turnunder on each edge and an overlap at the seam. Allow one width of the seam for a flat seam, two widths for a single-felled seam, and three widths for a double-felled seam.

(3) Fold the patch in half lengthwise, so that the left and right edges are even.

(4) Cut the top edge of the patch at a 22½° angle, cutting from the cut edges to the folded edge.

(5) With the patch still folded, cut along the folded edge, making two patches of the same size.

(6) Place one patch on the bottom ply of the seam, even with the edge. Double stitch the patch over the damage and cut away the damaged area one-eighth of an inch from the stitching.

(7) Place the other patch over the top ply of the seam, extending the patch one seam width beyond the seam. Double stitch the patch over the damage, and cut away the damaged area as in (6) above.

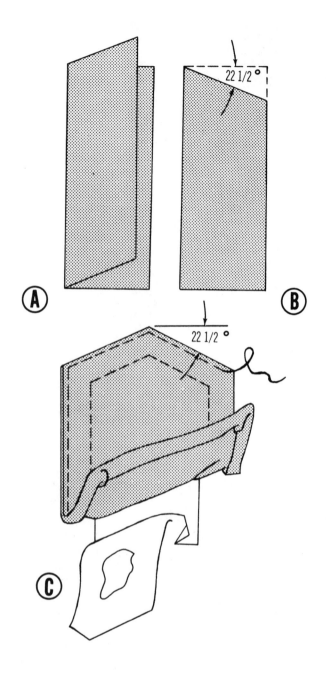

Figure 39. Watershed patch.

(1) The piece of patch material must be large enough to extend 2 inches on all sides of the damaged area, allowing for a ⅜-inch turn-under of the edges and for an overlap double the width of the seam.

(2) The patch is folded lengthwise, left over right, so that the left edge of the patch is short of the right edge, a distance double the width of the seam overlap.

(3) The top panel is overlapped on the turned-over edge of the bottom panel, and the single-felled seam is restitched.

(4) The patch is finished by a reinforcement tape stitched over the unfinished edge of the seam, care being taken that all overlapping ends face downward.

j. Eave Patches. A damaged tent eave is repaired with a top patch. The type of top patch depends on the location of the eave damage.

(1) *Eave-edge patch.* When damage occurs on or near the edge of an eave, repair it with a four-thickness patch (fig 29) extending for at least 2 inches on each side of the damaged area.

(2) *Eave-base patch.* When the damage extends into the eave-base stitching, repair it with an eave-base patch (watershed top patch) (fig 43). Apply an eave-base patch to a damaged eave as follows:

(*a*) Turn the tent inside out, and open the seams on all sides of the damaged area at least 6 inches.

(*b*) Turn the tent right side up and flatten the damaged area.

(*c*) Apply an overseam patch (*h* above).

(*d*) Restitch the eave seam as shown in figure 43.

k. Seam-to-Seam Patch. Extensive damage between seams is repaired with a seam-to-seam patch. This patch is a shingle-type patch, which sheds water away from the top and bottom patch seams. The procedure for making the seam-to-seam patch (fig 44) is as follows:

(1) Square the damaged area from seam to seam (A).

(2) Open the seams 2 inches above and below the damaged area (B).

(3) Cut away the damage on the marks used to square the damaged area (C).

(4) Cut a patch 1½ inches larger on all sides than the area cut away. This excess allows 1 inch for each seam and one-half of an inch for turning under the edge on all sides of the patch.

(5) Tuck the top edge of the patch under the top edge of the panel (D) 1½ inches. Fold the tope edge of the panel under one-half of an inch, and sew it with two rows of stitches, sew-

(8) Fold the extended edge of the top-ply patch under, making sure the edge is even with the original seam. Overlap the top ply of the seam on the bottom ply, and restitch the seam, backstitching at each break.

i. Reinforced-Seam Patch. The most common reinforced seam used in canvas repair is the single-felled seam with a reinforcing strip of material, such as tape, light webbing, or canvas. When a hole or tear occurs on a seam of this type, it is repaired with a reinforced-seam patch. The basic construction of the reinforced-seam patch (fig 42) is the same as that of the over-seam patch, with the following exceptions:

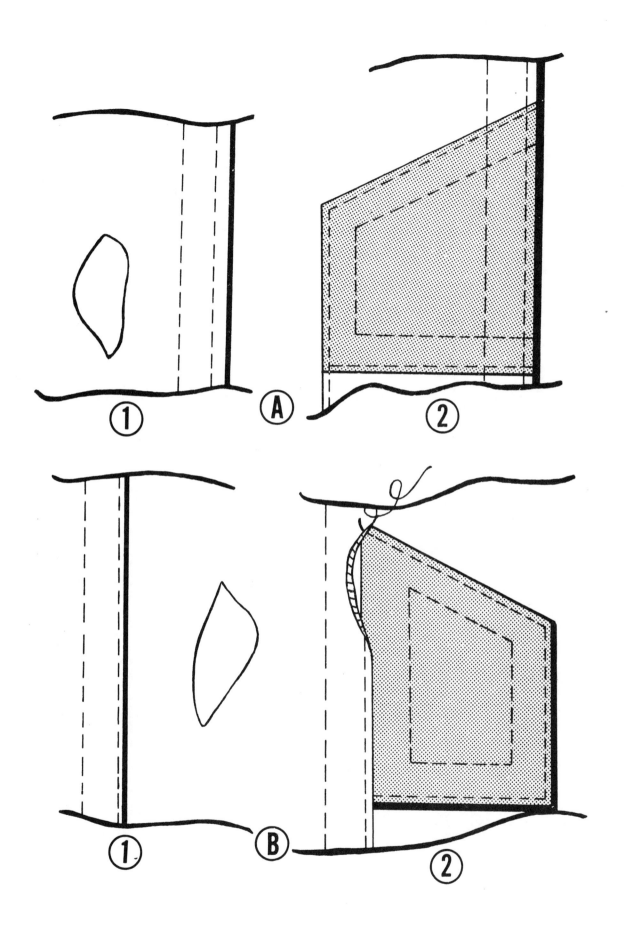

Figure 40. Patches near seam.

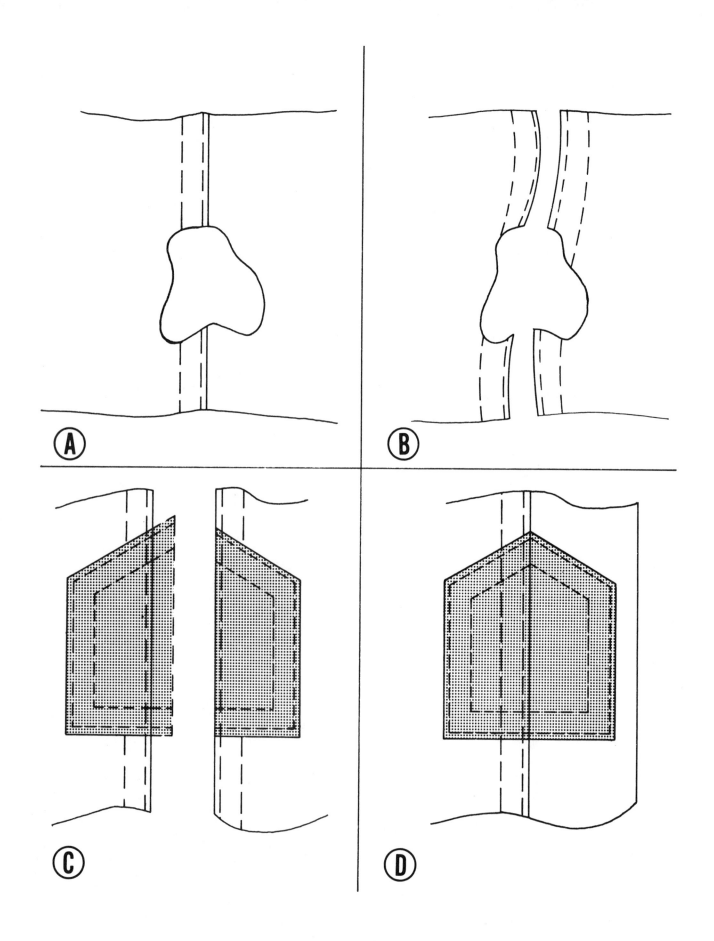

Figure 41. Watershed overseam patch.

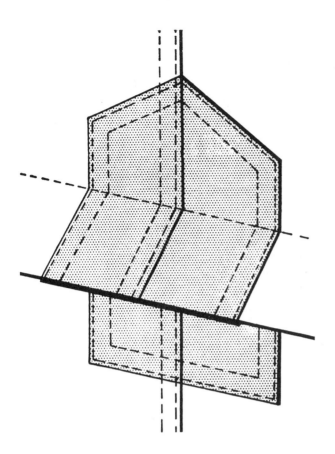

Figure 42. Reinforced-seam patch.

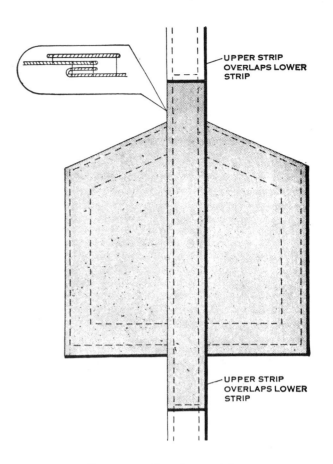

UPPER STRIP
OVERLAPS LOWER
STRIP

UPPER STRIP
OVERLAPS LOWER
STRIP

Figure 43. Eave-base patch.

ing from one edge of the panel to the other edge.

(6) Lap the bottom edge of the patch over the bottom edge of the panel (E) 1½ inches. Fold the bottom edge of the patch under one-half of an inch and sew it in place, following the same procedures for sewing the top edge.

(7) Sew the two side seams as shown in figure 45. Make sure there are no puckers and that seams are backstitched (F).

Note. If the patching material is the same width as the panel being patched, allow only 1½ inch larger on top and bottom of the patch. This will allow 1 inch for top and bottom seams and ½ inch for turning under the raw edges.

l. Tent Patches. The types of tent patches at typical locations on a tent are shown in figure 46. These patches (*a* through *k* above) are specifically designed to divert water from the openings and seams and prevent it from gathering in pockets and rotting the stitching.

m. Paulin Patches. Patches used for the repair of paulins are similar to those used for tent repair. The difference is that some of the patches are triangular so that water can shed easily when the paulin is laid over flat or irregular objects. All damaged areas are trimmed away after the patches are sewed (fig 47).

14. Re-treating Tents and Paulins

Tents and paulins are made primarily of fire-, water-, and mildew-resistant materials. To increase their durability, tents and paulins should be re-treated, as required, with pigmented, paste-form, solvent-type, mildew-resistant, textile preservative compound

a. Canvas. Procedures for re-treating tent canvas are described below. Paulin canvas should be re-treated by adapting these procedures.

(1) Make sure the tent is dry. Remove dirt, oil, and grease stains.

(2) Re-treat the tent while it is erected or raised with a hoist, as appropriate.

(3) Stir the compound thoroughly, and then dilute it with an equal amount of drycleaning solvent, continuing the stirring. Stir it again just before using it. One gallon of diluted compound is enough to cover about 10 square yards of fabric surface (one coat).

(4) Apply the compound by brush or spray gun. If a spray gun is used, the operator should wear utility clothing, a respirator, and a helmet liner.

(5) Apply the compound to the tent top first. Then pull the tent up off the ground, and finish the operation. Apply the compound generously to patches and newly repaired areas.

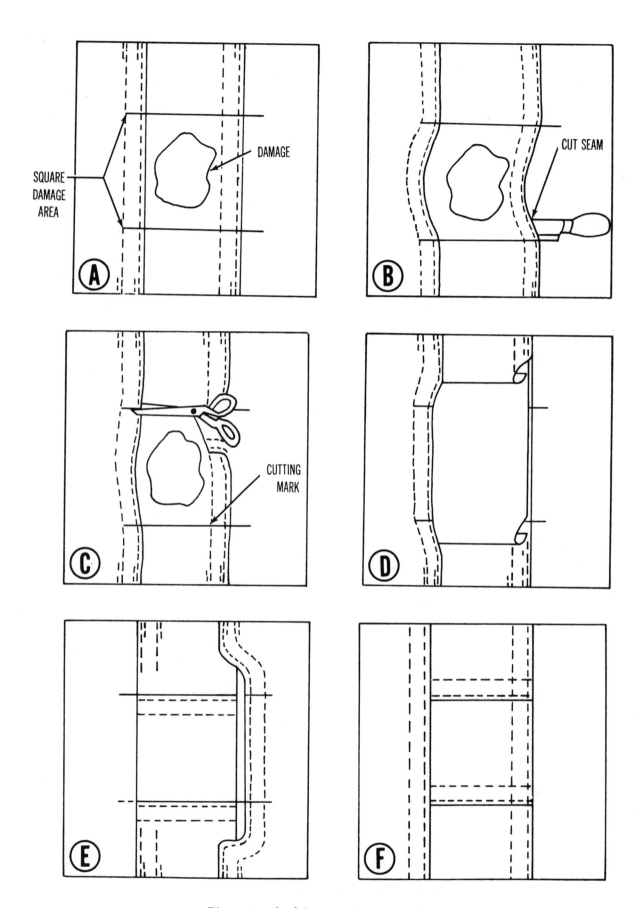

Figure 44. Applying seam-to-seam patch.

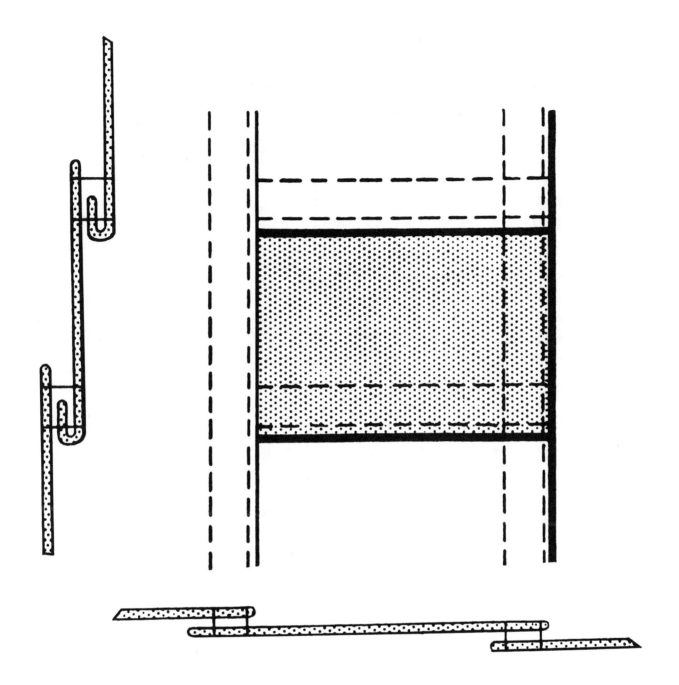

Figure 45. Completed seam-to-seam patch.

(6) Let the tent dry. Drying times depend on the drying method used.

Warning: **If the compound, which contains a strong fungicide, is handled carelessly, it may enter the body through the skin or through inhalation. Therefore, after treating tents, personnel who used the compound should wash thoroughly. Fire precautions are necessary during application because the compound is flammable.**

b. Seams. Tent and paulin seams may require further treatment. The procedures for re-treating seams are as follows:

(1) Make sure the tent or paulin is dry. Remove dirt, oil, and grease stains.

(2) Spread the seams on a hard, flat surface.

(3) Mix the compound as in *a*(3) above.

(4) Apply the first of two coats of the diluted compound to the outside of every seam. Use a 4-inch-wide, stiff paintbrush to apply a brushwide stripe of the compound over the length of each seam.

(5) Give special attention to all webbing attachments and turnbacks of webbing reinforcements.

(6) Normally, air-dry the first coat for at

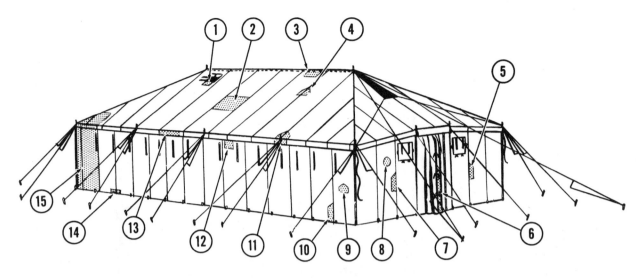

1 Stovepipe-opening patch
2 Seam-to-seam patch
3 Rectangular overridge patch
4 Watershed overseam patch
5 Patch near seam, bottom ply
6 Patch for replacing a row of grommets
7 Patch near seam, top ply
8 Cement patch
9 Watershed patch at midpanel
10 Watershed patch near hem
11 Eave-base patch
12 Rectangular patch under eave
13 Eave edge patch
14 Edge grommet patch
15 Corner replacement

Figure 46.   Tent patches applied to tent.

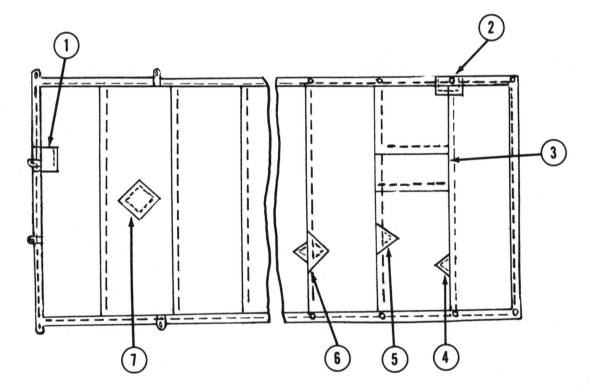

1 Tie-loop patch
2 Grommet patch
3 Full width patch at midpanel
4 Watershed patch at seam—bottom ply
5 Watershed patch at seam—top ply
6 Watershed patch at seam—top ply and bottom ply
7 Watershed patch at midpanel

Figure 47.   Paulin patches applied to paulin.

least 4 hours before applying the second coat. The 4-hour drying period may be reduced by using hot air to drive the solvent out of the compound.

(7) When the first coat is dry to the touch, apply the second coat, and allow the seams to dry at least 24 hours before erecting or repacking the tent or paulin.

CHAPTER 4
REPAIR OF EQUIPMENT PARTS

Section I. TACK-BUTTONS AND BUTTONHOLES

15. Tack-Buttons

The button commonly used on canvas and webbing items is the tack-button (fig 48), a button consisting of two parts, a button and a tack. This type of button may be attached either by hand or by a tack-button machine.

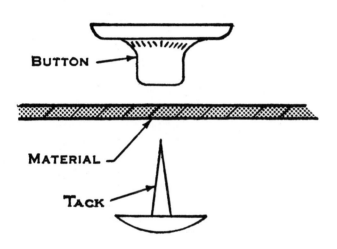

Figure 48. Installation of tack-button.

a. Installing Tack-Button by Hand. A tack-button is hand fastened to the material as follows:

(1) Insert the tack through the material from the underside.

(2) Place the button on the tack point.

(3) Place the unclinched parts, tack head up, on a smooth, hard surface.

b. Installing Tack-Button by Machine. Machine fastening a tack-button to the material differs from the hand fastening in only one operation. Instead of the tack-button being clinched to the material with the hammer and a smooth surface, the tack, material, and button are placed between the flat punch and die of a tack-button machine and are pressed together by operation of a foot lever.

16. Buttonholes

Damaged buttonholes may be repaired or replaced (fig 49) in the following ways:

a. Cut away the damaged material, and apply a top patch. The top patch may be a piece of salvaged material containing a buttonhole (A) or a piece of plain material in which the buttonhole has to be made.

b. Add a new piece of material to the back of the buttonhole strip (B), and rework the old buttonhole to the new material, using the buttonhole stitch (fig 50).

c. Cut away the damaged buttonhole strip, and attach a new backing and a new facing, taking care to seam the backing to the facing before folding over and top-stitch into place (C, fig 49). Make a new buttonhole.

(4) Clinch the tack and button to the material with a hammer blow hard enough to secure the parts to the material without damaging the fabric or the button.

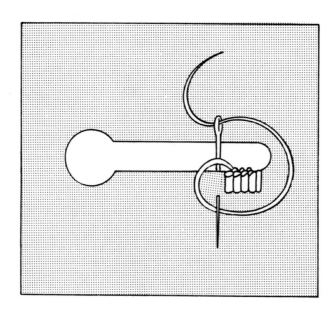

Figure 50. Buttonhole stitch.

Section II. GROMMETS

17. General

Metal grommets are used to reinforce and protect fabric at points where grommet holes are made to hold ropes, lines, spindles, and sometimes webbing straps. Grommets are either handworked or die inserted. When a grommet pulls away from tent fabric, the grommet and sometimes the fabric supporting the grommet must be replaced. When the damage to the fabric surrounding the grommet is slight, an emergency repair may be made by removing the old grommet and inserting a larger grommet. The repair should not be made with a larger grommet unless there is ample unweakened material around the grommet area to give adequate support. Should it be necessary to replace the supporting material, a grommet-support patch should be applied as shown in figures 27 through 29. A handworked grommet is replaced by resewing an iron ring to the grommet hole. A die-inserted grommet is replaced by installing a new brass die-inserted grommet.

18. Handworked Grommet

A handworked grommet is an iron ring hand sewn to the grommet hole. Because this type of grommet withstands great strain, it is commonly used on heavy tents. If a handworked grommet is to be resewn, the fabric around the grommet hole must be undamaged. In addition to hand-sewing tools and materials, the following are needed: iron ring, cutting punch rawhide mallet, fid (shelter-half tent pin or pointed stick), and heavy woodblock with enough end grain to provide a surface for

cutting the grommet hole. All but the fid and woodblock are in the tentage repair kit. The tentage repair kit has ½-, ¾-, and 1-inch iron grommet rings. Install a handworked grommet as follows:

a. If a new grommet hole must be made, lay the material, top side up, on the woodblock (end-grain surface), and cut a grommet hole with a cutting punch (fig 51). Use the ½-inch cutting punch for the ½- and ¾-inch rings and the ⁹⁄₁₆-inch cutting punch for the 1-inch ring. If the old grommet hole is used, select a ring with an inside diameter larger than that of the grommet hole.

Note. In a fixed repair shop several sizes of cutting punches are available. The repairman should select the appropriate size for the ring used.

b. Center the ring over the grommet hole (fig 52).

c. Pierce holes for stitching, not to exceed one-sixteenth of an inch in diameter, about one-eighth of an inch from the outer edge of the centered ring, making equally spaced piercings around the ring, as shown in figure 53.

d. Cut and wax ample thread (fig 6) to provide four strands for stitching.

e. Thread a sailmaker's needle to make a four-strand thread (fig 8), and knot the ends.

f. Twist the four strands together, rewax the thread (fig 9), and cut off the knotted end.

g. Begin handworking the grommet by inserting the needle one-eighth of an inch from the outside edge (through the pierced holes) of the ring

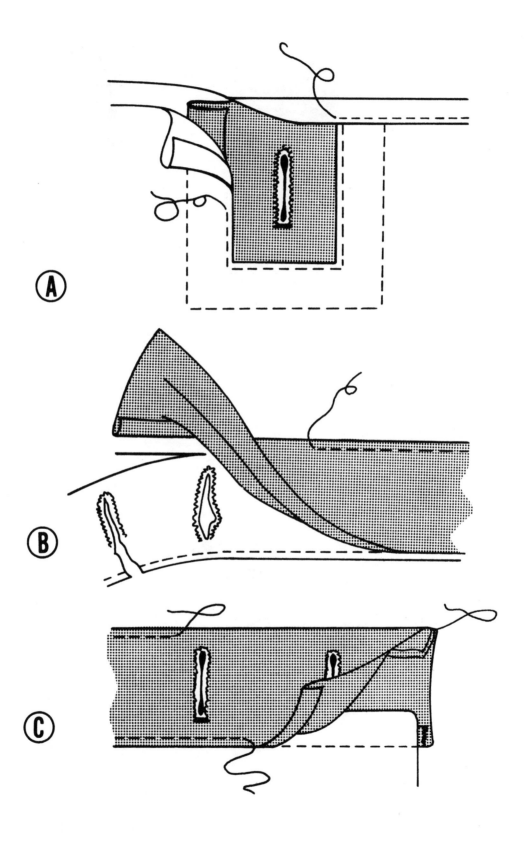

Figure 49. Common ways to replace buttonholes.

Figure 51.   Cutting grommet hole for handworked grommet.

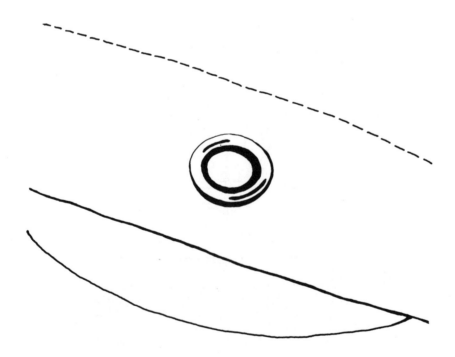

Figure 52.   Grommet ring centered over grommet hole.

and drawing the threads through until a ½-inch end remains (fig 54).

h. Secure the thread ends along the outer edge of the grommet ring by bringing the needle through the grommet hole and inserting it for a second stitch (fig 55).

i. Handwork the grommet to the material with a round stitch (B, fig 4), working clockwise around the grommet ring.

j. Finish the handworking of the grommet by passing the needle under the last two stitches (fig 56) and drawing the thread tight.

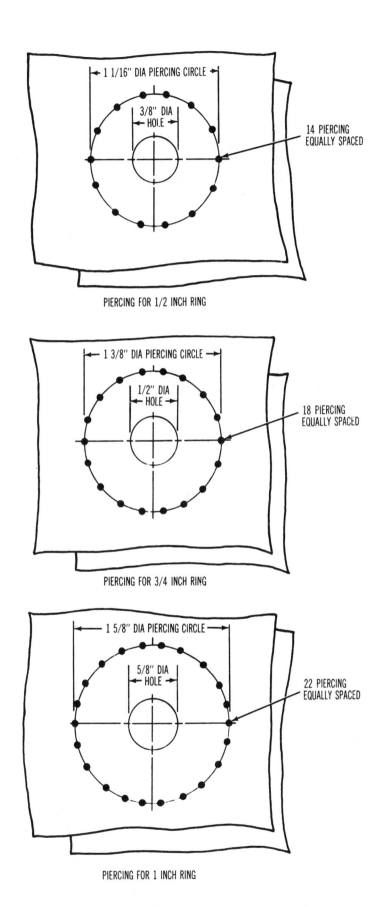

1 1/16" DIA PIERCING CIRCLE

3/8" DIA HOLE

14 PIERCING EQUALLY SPACED

PIERCING FOR 1/2 INCH RING

1 3/8" DIA PIERCING CIRCLE

1/2" DIA HOLE

18 PIERCING EQUALLY SPACED

PIERCING FOR 3/4 INCH RING

1 5/8" DIA PIERCING CIRCLE

5/8" DIA HOLE

22 PIERCING EQUALLY SPACED

PIERCING FOR 1 INCH RING

Figure 53. Piercing patterns for handworked grommets.

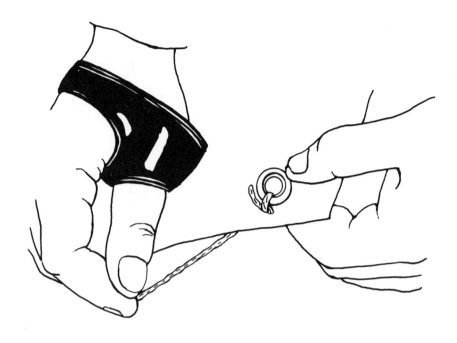

*Figure 54. Grommet ring, showing location of ½-inch
thread end.*

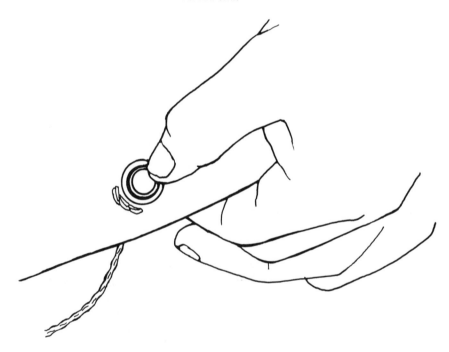

*Figure 55. Method of securing end of the thread for
handworked grommet.*

k. Cut the thread, leaving a ½-inch free end.

l. Flatten the stitching by pressing a wood fid
or shelter-half tent pin into the grommet hole,
first from the top and then from the bottom (fig
57).

19. Die-Inserted Grommet

A die-inserted grommet is a two-part brass grommet consisting of a male part, the barrel, and a
female part, the washer. The barrel is smooth, but
the washer has spurs that grip the material. The
two parts, with the fabric between them, are
clinched together by means of a punch-and-die
set. The materials and tools needed for the die-
inserted grommet are a brass grommet, a punch-
and-die set, a cutting punch, a rawhide mallet,

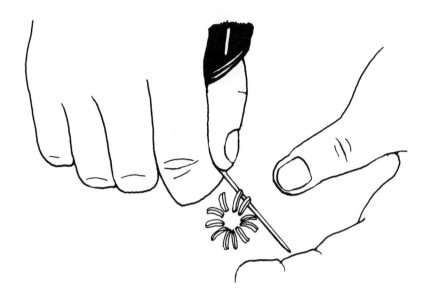

Figure 56. Method of finishing the stitching for handworked grommet.

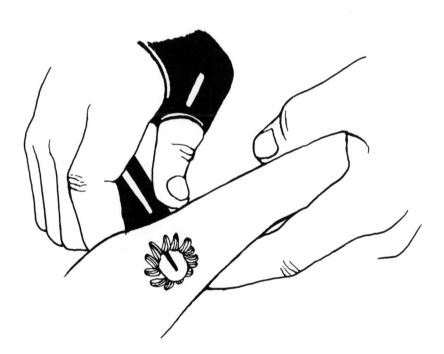

Figure 57. Handworked grommet, showing stitching being flattened.

and a woodblock with enough end grain to provide a surface for cutting a grommet hole. All but the woodblock are in the tentage repair kit. The tentage repair kit has No. 4 brass grommets, with an inside diameter of one-half of an inch, and No. 5 brass grommets, with an inside diameter of five-eighths of an inch. Install a die-inserted grommet as follows:

a. If it is necessary to cut a new grommet hole, lay the material on the woodblock (end-grain surface), or lead block, and cut the hole with the cutting punch (fig 58). Use the ½-inch cutting punch for the No. 4 grommet hole, and the ⁹⁄₁₆-inch cutting punch for the No. 5 grommet hole.

b. Insert the grommet barrel into the hole in

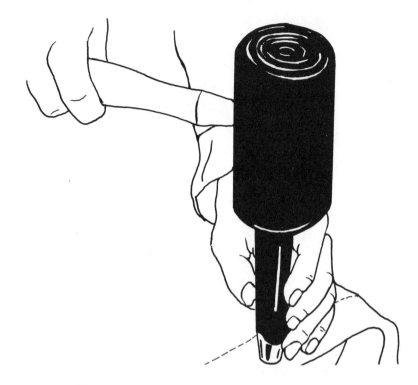

Figure 58. Cutting grommet hole for die-inserted grommet.

Figure 59. Placing barrel of die-inserted grommet on grommet die.

the material so that the flange of the barrel is on the underside of the material.

c. Place the inserted barrel with the flange resting on the grommet die (fig 59). Use the No. 4 die with the No. 4 grommet barrel, and the No. 5 die with the No. 5 grommet barrel.

d. Place the grommet washer, spurs down, over the grommet barrel (fig 60).

e. Insert the grommet punch into the **grommet barrel,** and with a mallet blow, clinch them together (fig 61). If properly done, the barrel edge will have a smooth roll (fig 62). **Failure to use the proper punch and die may cause faulty clinching of the grommet and may split the barrel edge.**

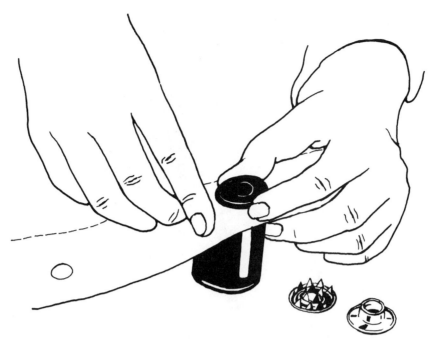

Figure 60.   Placing washer of die-inserted grommet over grommet barrel.

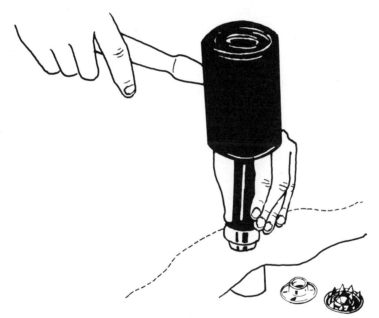

Figure 61.   Clinching die-inserted grommet.

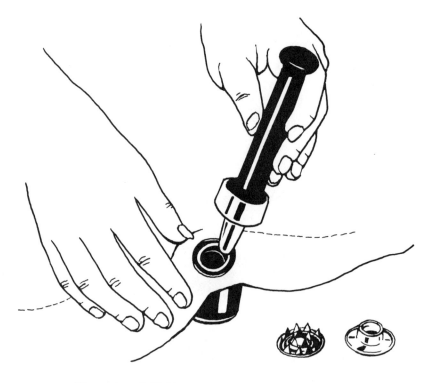

Figure 62. Rolled barrel edge of die-inserted grommet.

Section III. SNAP FASTENERS AND SLIDE FASTENERS

20. Replacing Style 1 Snap Fastener

The style 1 snap fastener consists of a male section and a female section. The female section has two parts, the socket and the clinch plate. The male section also has two parts, the stud and the stud washer. The stud is made in two sizes, single and double. The double stud, which is twice as long as the single stud, can hold an additional ply of material.

a. Installing Female Section. The following parts and tools are needed for installing the female section of the style 1 snap fastener: style 1 snap fastener socket, style 1 snap fastener clinch plate, style 1 snap fastener socket punch, style 1 snap fastener socket anvil, wood or rawhide mallet, and lead block. Install the female section of the style 1 snap fastener (fig 63) as follows:

(1) Place the material on a lead block, centering the area in which the socket is to be inserted (fig 64).

(2) Center the socket punch over the fastener location, and with a mallet blow, make a center hole for the socket opening and holes for the socket prongs.

Note. The irregular placement of the socket-prong holes around the center hole make it imperative that the socket punch be set properly before making the cut. A properly inserted socket always has the smaller prongs (in width) toward the outer edge of the item being repaired (fig 65).

(3) Insert the socket into the prepared holes, with prongs extending through to the underside of the material.

(4) Fit the clinch plate on the socket prongs.

(5) Place the loose fastener section, prongs up, on the style 1 snap fastener socket anvil. With a riveting hammer, or with the top end of the socket punch, bend the socket prongs toward the center, flattening the prongs against the clinch plate until the plate and socket are securely clinched to the material.

b. Installing Male Section. The following parts and tools are needed for installing the male section of the style 1 snap fastener: style 1 snap fastener stud, style 1 snap fastener stud washer, style 1 snap fastener stud set, style 1 snap fastener stud anvil, six-tube revolving belt punch, and a wood or rawhide mallet. Install the male section of the style 1 snap fastener (fig 66) as follows:

(1) Cut a hole in the material, using a tube of the revolving punch, small enough for a tight fit around the stud barrel.

(2) Insert the stud barrel into the hole in the material, making certain that the prong of the stud extends in the direction necessary to receive the socket section of the fastener.

(3) Place the inserted stud, prong down, on the anvil.

(4) Fit the washer over the stud barrel.

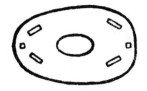

STYLE 1 SNAP FASTENER CLINCH PLATE

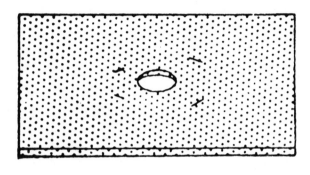

MATERIAL

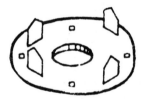

STYLE 1 SNAP FASTENER SOCKET

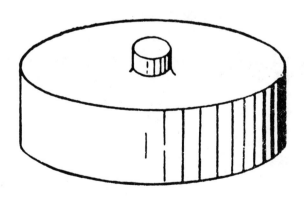

STYLE 1 SNAP FASTENER SOCKET ANVIL

Figure 63.   Installation of style 1 snap fastener socket.

(5) Place the style 1 snap fastener stud set on the stud barrel, and with a mallet blow, clinch the stud and washer to the material.

21. Replacing Style 2 Snap Fastener

The style 2 snap fastener has a female section consisting of a cap and a socket, and a male section consisting of a stud and a post.

a. *Installing Female Section.* The following parts and tools are needed for installing the female section of the style 2 snap fastener: style 2 snap fastener cap, style 2 snap fastener socket, style 2 snap fastener cap-and-post set, style 2 snap fastener cap anvil, six-tube revolving belt punch, and a wood or rawhide mallet. Install the female section of the style 2 snap fastener (fig 67) as follows:

(1) Cut a hole in the material, using a tube of the revolving punch, small enough for a tight fit around the barrel of the cap.

(2) Insert the barrel of the cap through the hole in the material.

Note. The female section of the style 2 snap fastener is always installed in the outer part of the item being repaired, with the cap on the top side of the material.

(3) Place the inserted cap, barrel up, on the anvil.

(4) Fit the socket over the barrel of the cap.

(5) Place the cap-and-post set on the barrel of the cap, and with a mallet blow, clinch the cap and socket to the material.

b. *Installing Male Section.* The following parts and tools are needed for installing the male section of the style 2 snap fastener: style 2 snap fastener stud, style 2 snap fastener post, style 2 snap fastener cap-and-post set, style 2 snap fastener post anvil, six-tube revolving belt punch, and a wood or rawhide mallet. Install the male section of the style 2 snap fastener (fig 68) as follows:

(1) Cut a hole in the material using a tube of the revolving punch, small enough for a tight fit around the barrel of the post.

(2) Insert the barrel of the post through the hole in the material from the underside of the material.

(3) Place the inserted post, barrel up, on the anvil.

(4) Fit the stud over the barrel of the post.

(5) Place the cap-and-post set on the barrel of the post, and with a mallet blow, clinch the post and stud to the material.

22. Slide Fasteners

Damaged slide fasteners on tents or other canvas items are replaced in accordance with technical manuals for the items. When these manuals are

not available or do not apply, replace fasteners using appropriate procedures below.

a. *Separable-Type Fastener.* Either side or both sides of the fastener may be replaced. Replace a separable-type slide fastener (fig 69) as follows:

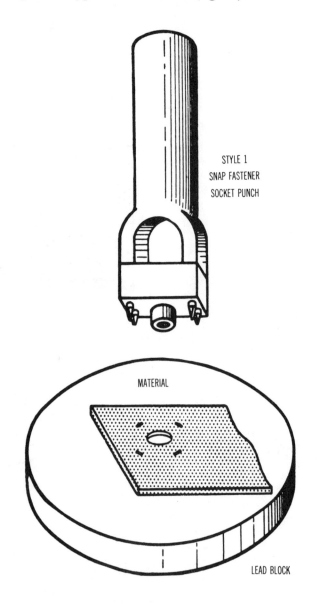

STYLE 1
SNAP FASTENER
SOCKET PUNCH

MATERIAL

LEAD BLOCK

Figure 64. Cutting holes in material for installation of style 1 snap fastener socket.

(1) Select a fastener of the correct length and type.

(2) Place the new slide fastener over the unserviceable fastener. Draw index marks across the slide fastener tapes and on the material of the item.

(3) Remove the damaged fastener from the item.

(4) When replacing only one side of a fastener, seat the pin in the box stop, place the fastener

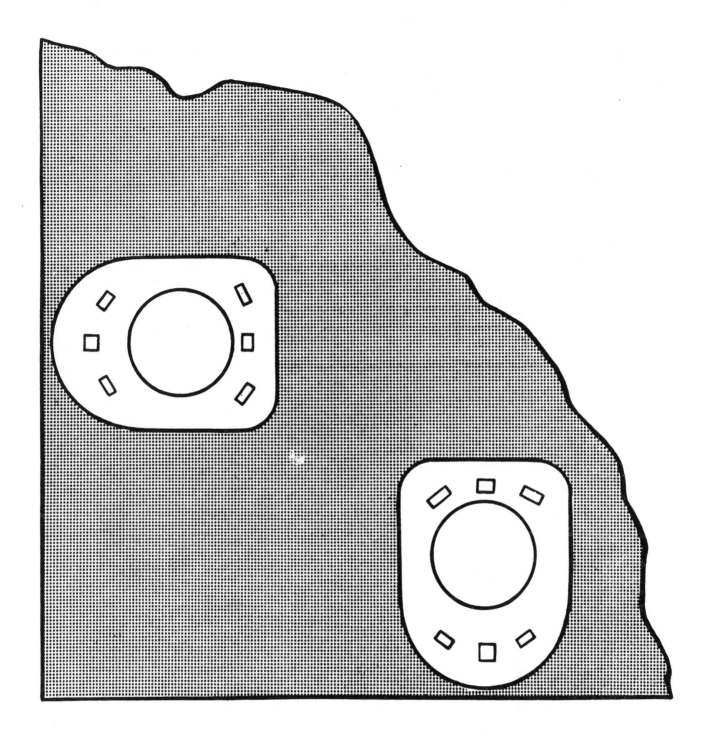

Figure 65. Proper position of style 1 snap fastener socket.

tape on the material so that the index marks match, and sew the side of the fastener in place with one or more rows of stitches. The stitching should be at least three-sixteenths of an inch from the scoops or a sufficient distance to allow free movement of the slider.

(5) When replacing both sides of a fastener, match the index marks on the tapes with the marks on the item. Sew the tapes to the items as in (4) above.

(6) Trim the top ends of the tapes, turn the ends under, and stitch them in place.

b. *Nonseparable-Type Fastener.*

(1) Select the fastener of the correct length and type.

(2) Close the new fastener, and proceed as in *a*(2) and (3) above.

(3) Sew the new fastener in place as in *a*(5) and (6) above.

c. *Touch-and-Close-Type Fastener.* For some re-

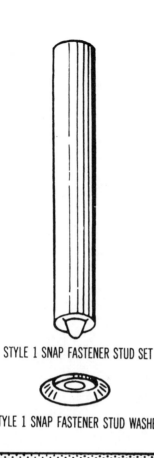

STYLE 1 SNAP FASTENER STUD SET

STYLE 1 SNAP FASTENER STUD WASHER

MATERIAL

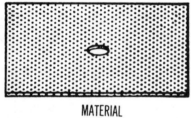

BARREL OF STUD

STYLE 1 SNAP FASTENER STUD

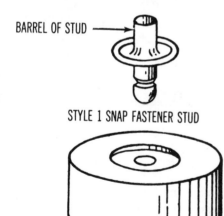

STYLE 1 SNAP FASTENER STUD ANVIL

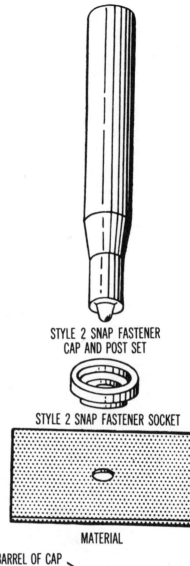

STYLE 2 SNAP FASTENER
CAP AND POST SET

STYLE 2 SNAP FASTENER SOCKET

MATERIAL

BARREL OF CAP

STYLE 2 SNAP FASTENER CAP

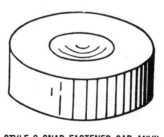

STYLE 2 SNAP FASTENER CAP ANVIL

Figure 66. Installation of style 1 snap fastener stud.   *Figure 67. Installation of style 2 snap fastener socket.*

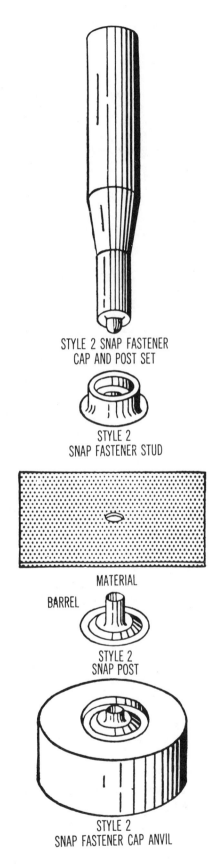

STYLE 2 SNAP FASTENER
CAP AND POST SET

STYLE 2
SNAP FASTENER STUD

MATERIAL

BARREL

STYLE 2
SNAP POST

STYLE 2
SNAP FASTENER CAP ANVIL

Figure 68.   Installation of style 2 snap fastener stud.

pairs, slide fasteners may be replaced with touch-and-close-type fasteners. This type of fastener has two tapes. One tape is a matted nylon material, and the other tape is a material with many tiny nylon hooks. The hooks engage the matted material to make a firm closure.

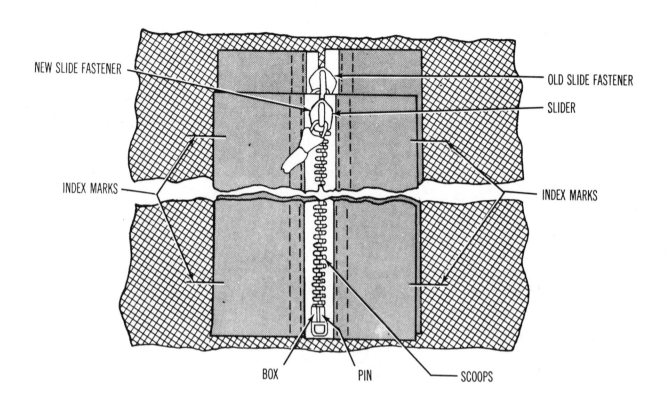

Figure 69. Method of index marking for slide fastener replacement.

Section IV. LINES AND TENT LINE SLIPS

23. Lines

Lines, or ropes, used on canvas and webbing items may be of manila, sisal, cotton, or jute. When they become badly worn, frayed, or mildewed, they must be replaced. The replacement rope and the method of fastening must be similar to the original construction. To replace lines properly, the repairman must know basic rope structure, rope knotting, and rope splicing.

Special attention should be given to those knots and splices (fig 70) commonly used in canvas and webbing repair.

a. *Regular Eye Splice.* When the end of a line requires a permanent loop for attaching hardware or for fastening grommets, the loop is generally made by eye splicing (A).   Insure a neat, close-fitting job by giving each strand at least three tucks to splice the eye securely and by rolling the finished splice between the hands or under the foot.

b. *Sailmaker's Eye Splice.* The sailmaker's eye splice (B), a splice following the lay of the rope, is used when the eye is to be sewn to canvas. This splice is started in the same manner as the regular eye splice, but the remaining tucks follow the lay of the rope.

c. *Tied Eye.* On some items having cotton braided rope, the eye is made by tying (C).

d. *Short Splice.* The short splice (D) is the strongest and the most secure way to join two ropes. Although it is stronger than the long splice, it increases the diameter of the rope, so that the spliced part of the rope may be unable to pass through a bull's eye, through a fair lead, or over the sheave of a block.

e. *Long Splice.* The long splice (E) is also used to join two ropes. Although it is weaker than the short splice and requires more rope, it does not appreciably increase the diameter of the rope. It can run through a bull's eye or over the sheave of a block without jamming.

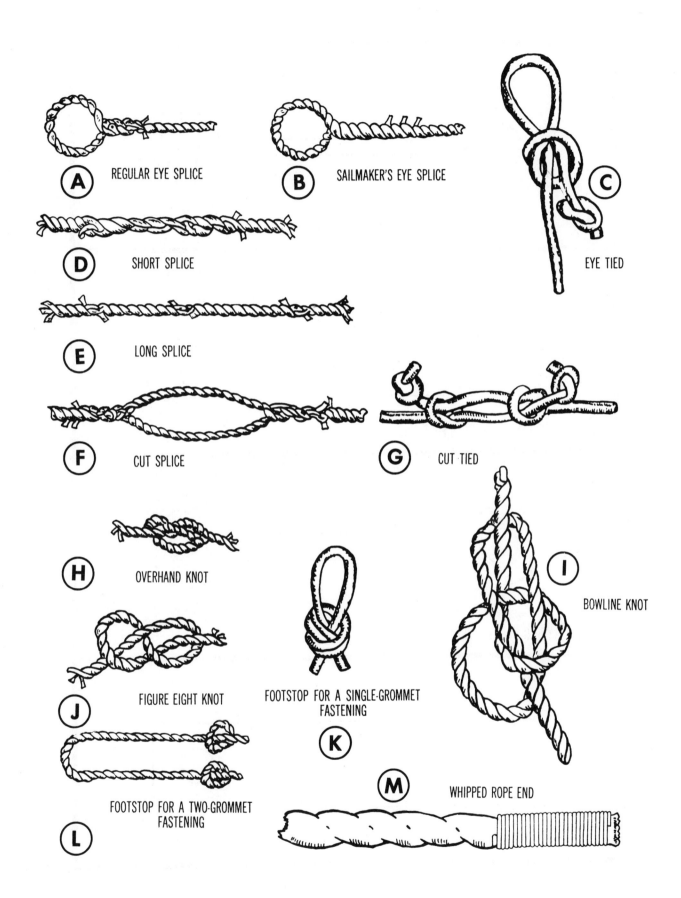

A REGULAR EYE SPLICE

B SAILMAKER'S EYE SPLICE

C EYE TIED

D SHORT SPLICE

E LONG SPLICE

F CUT SPLICE

G CUT TIED

H OVERHAND KNOT

I BOWLINE KNOT

J FIGURE EIGHT KNOT

K FOOTSTOP FOR A SINGLE-GROMMET FASTENING

L FOOTSTOP FOR A TWO-GROMMET FASTENING

M WHIPPED ROPE END

Figure 70. Knots and splices.

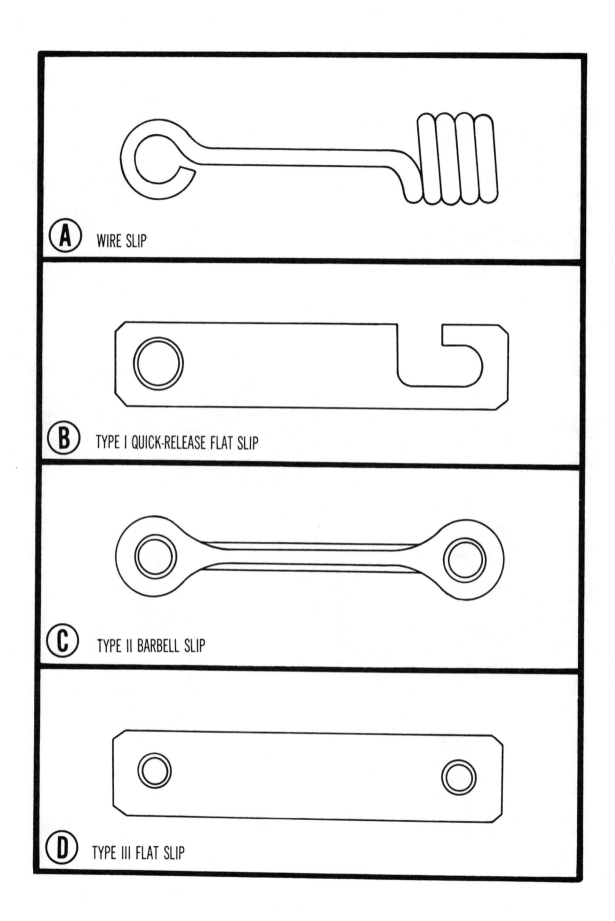

A WIRE SLIP

B TYPE I QUICK-RELEASE FLAT SLIP

C TYPE II BARBELL SLIP

D TYPE III FLAT SLIP

Figure 71.   Tent line slips.

f. Cut Splice. The cut splice (F) is the splicing together of two ropes, forming an eye at the splice. The rope ends pass each other the distance of the desired opening, and then each end tucks into the body of the other rope in the same manner that the end of the regular eye splice tucks into the rope. A cut splice is usually used in a double guy line, the cut being set over the pole spindle.

g. Tied Cut. For joining cotton braided rope, the tied cut (G) may be used.

h. Overhand Knot. The overhand knot (H) is used to keep an end from slipping through an eye or grommet.

i. Bowline Knot. The bowline knot (I) is used to form a loop that cannot slip.

j. Figure-Eight Knot. The figure-eight knot (J) is used to prevent a line from slipping through a grommet.

k. Footstop for a Single-Grommet Fastening. This type of footstop is made by looping a footstop line and securing the open ends with a single overhand knot (K).

l. Footstop for a Two-Grommet Fastening. This type of footstop is made by tying an overhand knot at each end of the footstop line (L).

m. Whipped Rope End. Whipping (M) is binding the end of a rope with cord to prevent the rope end from raveling. Whipping is always made against the lay of the rope, the turns being worked toward the end of the rope.

24. Tent Line Slips

There are four types of tent line slips (fig 71). These devices are used to adjust eave lines, or guy lines.

a. Wire Slip. This slip (A), made of ³⁄₁₆-inch-diameter steel wire, is 4 inches long. The wire is coiled like a spring at one end and looped to form an eye at the other end. Install a wire slip as follows:

(1) Reeve one end of the eave line through the coil end of the slip, reeving from the inside of the coil to the outside end, and draw about 2 feet of the line through the coil.

(2) Continuing with the same end, reeve the line through the eave grommet, reeving from the roof side to the wall side, and bring the end of the line through the eye of the slip.

(3) Secure the slip to the line by finishing the line end with an overhand knot.

b. Type I Quick-Release Flat Slip. This slip (B), made of magnesium alloy, has flat faces. It is 4 inches long and seven-eighths of an inch wide. It has a round hole at one end and a quick-release side opening at the other end. Install a type I quick-release flat slip as follows:

(1) Reeve one end of the eave line through the hole at one end of the slip, and draw about 2 feet of the line through the hole.

(2) Continuing with the same end, reeve the line through the eave grommet, reeving from the roof side to the wall side, and bring the end of the line through the quick-release side opening at the other end of the slip.

(3) Secure the slip to the line by finishing the line end with an overhand knot.

c. Type II Barbell Slip. This slip (C), made of cast magnesium alloy, is 4 inches long. It has a ⁷⁄₁₆-inch-diameter hole at each end. Its shape is similar to that of a barbell. Install a type II barbell slip as follows:

(1) Reeve one end of the eave line through the hole at one end of the slip, and draw about 2 feet of the line through the hole.

(2) Continuing with the same end, reeve the line through the eave grommet, reeving from the roof side to the wall side, and bring the line through the hole in the other end of the slip.

(3) Secure the slip to the line by finishing the line end with an overhand knot.

d. Type III Flat Slip. This slip (D) is similar to the type I quick-release flat slip (*b* above), except that it has a hole at each end and does not have the quick-release side opening. Install a type III flat slip by adapting the procedure in *c* above.

Section V. EYELETS, END CLIPS, RIVETS, AND OTHER HARDWARE

25. Eyelets

An eyelet is a small, metal, die-inserted grommet, similar to the large die-inserted grommet (para 19). It consists of a male part, the barrel, and a female part, the washer. The materials and tools needed for installing an eyelet are an eyelet barrel and washer, an eyelet set, an eyelet awl, a six-tube revolving belt punch, and a wood or rawhide mallet. Install an eyelet (fig 72) as follows:

a. Cut a hole in the material, using a tube of the revolving punch, small enough for a tight fit around the barrel of the eyelet.

b. Insert the barrel into the hole in the material so that the flange of the barrel is on the underside of the material.

c. Place the washer on the awl.

d. Place the inserted barrel, flange up, on the awl.

e. Place the eyelet set on the awl so that it rests

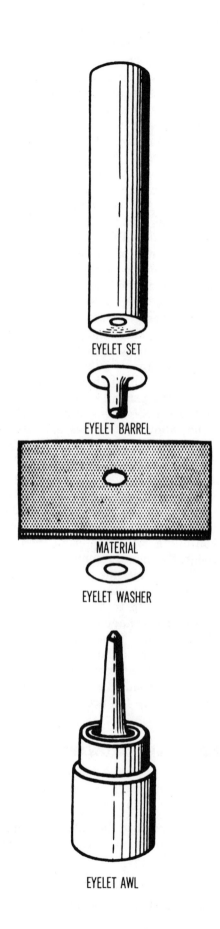

EYELET SET

EYELET BARREL

MATERIAL

EYELET WASHER

EYELET AWL

Figure 72. Installation of metal eyelet.

on the barrel, and with a mallet blow, clinch the barrel and washer to the material.

26. End Clips

End clips (fig 73) are metal tips used to protect the free, unfinished ends of webbing straps and to provide a solid tip for easy insertion into grommets or buckles. There are three types, the ball, the flat, and the end-buckle clip.

a. Ball-Type End Clip. The ball-type end clip (A) is so named because it has the appearance of a hollow metal ball before it is flattened to form an end clip. Actually, it is thimble shaped, with one side open to receive the end of the strap (A1). The proper method of attaching an end clip is to insert the strap in the clip, partially flatten the clip, straighten the strap to prevent curling, and then finish flattening the clip with a hammer or a machine designed for this purpose (A2).

b. Flat-Type End Clip. The flat-type end clip (B) is a flat strip of metal folded at the center, giving it a V-shaped appearance. The jaw ends of the clip usually have teeth to insure a firm grip on the fabric. The flat-type end clip may be clinched to the webbing either by hand using a hammer or by a machine designed for this purpose.

c. End-Buckle Clip. The end-buckle clip (C) is a flat-type end clip with a slot for holding a buckle or hook. The clip also has rivet holes so that it can be securely riveted in place after it is clinched.

27. Rivets

Brass and copper rivets are commonly used in the repair of canvas and webbing items (fig 74). The types generally used are belt rivets and tubular rivets.

a. Belt Rivets. Belt rivets (A), made of brass or copper, come in sizes 8, 10, 12, and 14 with lengths from 0.375 to 1.25 inches. Burs are made for each rivet size. To insure permanent riveting, the bur size should correspond to the rivet size.

b. Tubular Rivets. Tubular rivets (B), made of brass, have hollow shanks. They are about 0.145 inch in diameter and are supplied in 3/16- to 3/4-inch lengths. Tubular rivets may be used with caps. The tip of a tubular rivet is beveled on the inside so that it can be flanged into the rim of the cap.

c. Procedure for Installing Rivets. Install a belt rivet or a tubular rivet as follows:

(1) Cut a hole in the material, using a tube of the revolving punch, small enough for a tight fit around the rivet.

(2) Insert the rivet in the hole. Use a rivet long enough to take the bur or the cap, yet short enough to provide only the excess material necessary for peening or capping.

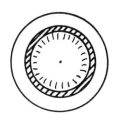
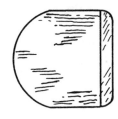

① BEFORE INSTALLATION

② AFTER INSTALLATION

A BALL-TYPE END CLIP

B FLAT-TYPE END CLIP

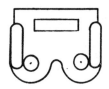

C END-BUCKLE CLIP

Figure 73.   End clips.

(3) Place the inserted rivet, head down, on a metal block.

(4) Fit the bur over the tip of the belt rivet, or fit the cap on the tubular rivet.

(5) Peen the tip of the belt rivet over the bur, using a ball-peen hammer. Clinch together the tubular rivet and the cap, using a plain-faced hammer.

28. Other Hardware

All metal trimmings and metal attachments on canvas and webbing items are referred to as hardware. Hardware items requiring special tools and individual procedures for installation are covered earlier in this chapter. Most other hardware items (fig 75) are attached by means of canvas or webbing loops known as chapes.

a. Rings. Circular metal pieces (1) are used as tie-tape fasteners, catches for snaphooks, and supports for handworked grommets.

b. Loops. Elongated metal rings (2) are used to hold webbing straps and also to form supports for handworked grommets.

c. D-Rings. Metal D-shaped rings (3) are used on canvas and webbing items to catch snaphooks and on tents to loop over pole spindles.

d. Triangles. Triangular metal pieces (4) are usually used on tents to carry canvas strain at pole spindles.

e. Links. Single, metal chain links are sometimes used where pole spindles pass through eaves. In a few instances they are used over pole spindles to support eave lines (5).

f. Squares. Square metal pieces (6) are used with webbing.

g. Double Hooks. Metal double hooks (7) are used to attach canvas equipment to the individual equipment belt.

h. Slide Loops. Metal slide loops with center bars (8) are used to adjust the length of straps.

i. Snaphooks. Snaphooks (9) are metal hooks with spring-steel snaps.

j. Wall D-Rings. Wall D-rings (10) are special-shaped D-rings used on assembly tents.

k. S-Hooks. These are metal S-shaped hooks (11).

l. Triangles With Hooks. Triangles with hooks (12) are used to connect fair-leads to webbing supports of tents (12).

m. Fair-Leads. Fair-leads (13) are magnesium block castings, 5½ by 1¼ inches, used to keep eave lines from chafing the canvas at tent eaves.

n. Buckles. Buckles (14, 15, and 16) are metal fasteners for strap ends.

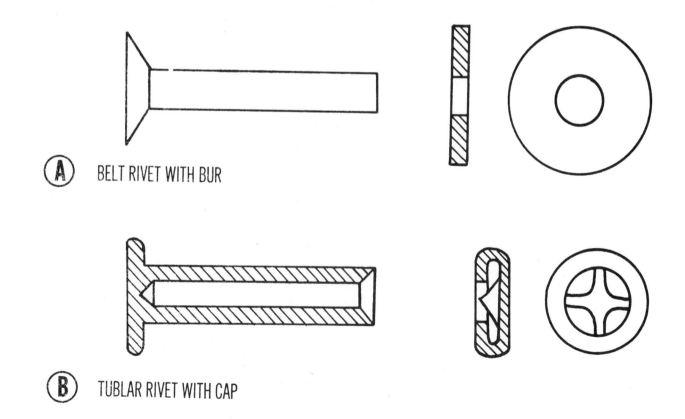

Ⓐ BELT RIVET WITH BUR

Ⓑ TUBLAR RIVET WITH CAP

Figure 74. Rivets.

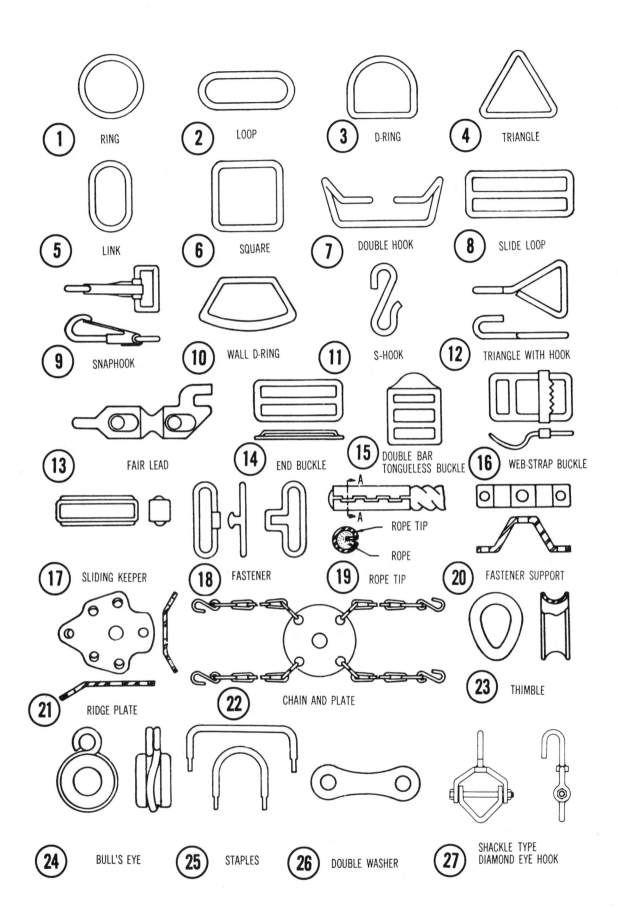

Figure 75.   Miscellaneous hardware.

o. Sliding Keepers. Sliding keepers (17) are metal loops used to hold straps in place.

p. Fasteners. Fasteners (18) are metal devices used to fasten belt ends.

q. Rope Tips. Rope tips (19) are metal caps used to finish rope ends.

r. Fastener Supports. U-shaped metal supports (20) are generally used to hold male sections of style 1 snap fasteners.

s. Ridge Plates. Metal ridge plates (21) are used with tents to protect and support the fabric about ridgepole spindles.

t. Chains and Plate. Metal plates with chains (22) are used at peaks of pyramidal tents.

u. Thimbles. Thimbles (23) are oval metal inserts that fit into splice eyes. They are used to reinforce the ends of tie lines.

v. Bull's-Eyes. Bull's eyes (24) are circular wooden blocks with a hole in the center. They are used to carry hoisting lines.

w. Staples. Staples (25) are U-shaped metal pieces with ends finished for riveting to material.

x. Double Washers. Double washers (26) are used with riveted staples to provide sufficient area coverage to prevent the staples from pulling through the fabric.

y. Shackle-Type Diamond Eye Hooks. These hooks (27) are constructed of heavy steel wire. Each hook has a lower shackle, an upper shackle with hooks, and a bolt with nut to connect the two shackles.

Section VI. CHAPES, LOOPS, BILLETS, STRAPS, AND HANDLES

29. Chapes

Chapes are canvas or webbing loops (fig 76) used to hold hardware to canvas and webbing (A). Chapes are designated as D-ring chapes, buckle chapes, and other names, according to the type of hardware they carry.

a. Fitting Chape Before Sewing. A chape may be fitted in the following ways:

(1) Insert a strip of webbing double the length of the proposed chape through the hardware so that the unfinished ends meet one above the other (B).

(2) Insert a strip of webbing double the length of the proposed chape through the hardware so that the top ply overlaps the bottom ply (C). Turn the top end under, butting it against the bottom end.

(3) Insert through the hardware a strip of webbing double the length of the proposed chape plus additional length for turning under the end (D). Turn the top end of webbing under so that it grips the bottom end.

(4) Insert a two-ply strip of webbing through the hardware. (A two-ply strip of webbing is made by folding in the center a piece four times the length of the proposed chape.) Fold again, setting the ends together, so that the folded end rests on two unfinished ends (E).

b. Sewing Chape in Place. Machine stitch a chape in place (fig 77) as follows:

(1) Place the work on the machine so that the presser foot rests on the upper right-hand corner of the chape with the hardware to the left.

(2) Sew in a clockwise direction the four sides of the stitching area (AB, BC, CD, DA (1)).

(3) Sew diagonally from corner to corner and again across the end (AC, CD (2)).

(4) Sew a second diagonal from corner to corner, crossing the first diagonal at the center of the stitching area (DB (3)).

(5) Finish with a row of stitching across the end (BA (3)).

c. Reinforcing Chape. Sometimes a chape is placed where it is subject to excessive tugging and pulling. At such a place, a simple chape with its small area of stitching would soon tear the chape-supporting fabric. A chape may be reinforced in the following ways:

(1) *Reinforcement patch.* To widen the stitching area and thereby increase the area of support, apply a reinforcement patch (fig 78) to the chape. This reinforcement is an additional piece of webbing set across the chape and sewed in place. The stitching in the center is crossed, and the ends are double stitched.

(2) *Reinforcement stitching.* Reinforce the chape by increasing the amount of machine stitching and by adding handstitches (fig 79). Run four rows of machine stitching parallel to the webbing at the nonhardware end and over each turned-under tip. Hand sew the hardware end in place, using four stitches around each side edge next to the hardware and five stitches around the end looped to the hardware.

30. Loops

Loops are often used on canvas and webbing equipment as line fastenings and strap retainers. Their construction is shown in figure 80.

a. Flat Loop. The flat loop (A) lies flat on the surface to which it is attached. It is made by cutting a piece of webbing the length of the proposed loop, plus material for turning under the ends. Each end is sewed with crossed rows of stitching.

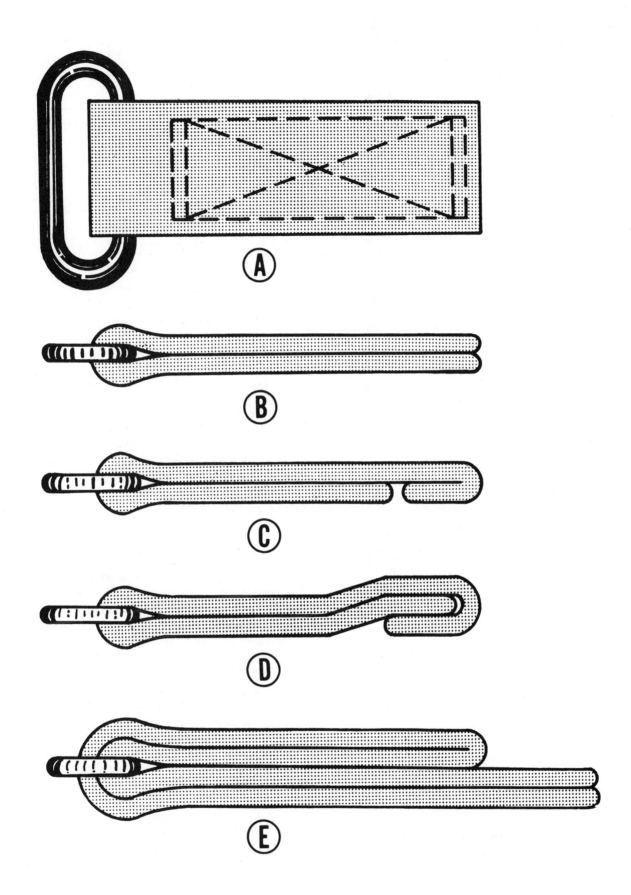

Figure 76.   Chapes, showing ways of folding webbing.

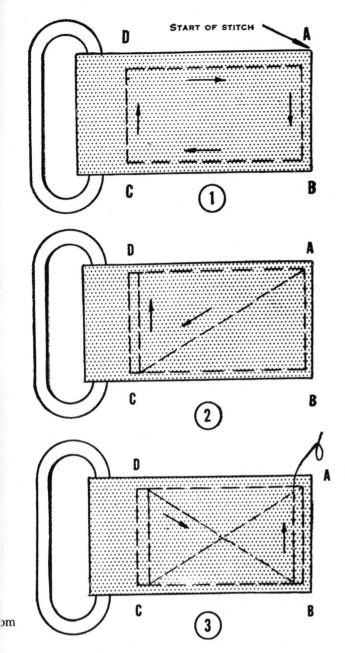

Figure 77. *Method of sewing chapes.*

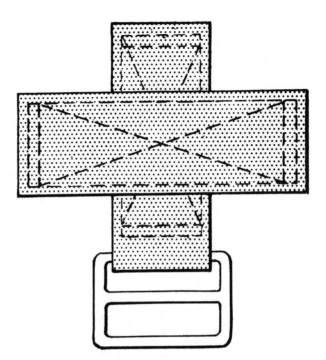

Figure 78. *Buckle chape with reinforcement patch.*

31. Billets

Straps that enter buckles are known as billets. A billet (fig 81) is made by cutting a piece of webbing the length of the desired billet, plus about three-fourths of an inch for turnunder. An end clip (para 26) is attached to one end, the other end is turned under, and the billet is sewed in place.

32. Straps

Webbing straps of various lengths, widths, and thicknesses are used on canvas and webbing equipment. The design of each strap is governed by the strap use. Except for overall dimensions, the main differences in strap construction are the designs of the strap ends. Construction of a typical strap ends (fig 82) is described below. The ends of a plain strap (*a* and *b* below) are the same width as the strap body. The ends of other straps (*c* through *h* below) are narrower than the strap body to fit smaller hardware.

a. Plain Tip End. The tip end (A) is merely a cut end of a strap. It is usually finished by attaching an end clip (para 26) to it.

b. Plain Loop End. The webbing end is looped (A) through the buckle, ring, or similar hardware, the raw edge is turned under, and the end is sewed to the strap body.

c. Rolled Tip End. The webbing end is tapered (B) by rolling the edges to the centerline of the webbing, abutting the edges the length of the desired end, and then angling the folded-in edges to the outer edges of the strap body. The taper for

b. Short Loop. The short loop (B) extends a short distance from the surface to which it is attached. The base of the loop is bar tacked before the end tabs are sewed in place.

c. Two-Ply Long Loop. Where a long, strong loop is required, the loop is made with two plies of webbing (C). The two plies are first stitched together with a row of stitching along each edge and are then bar tacked and sewed in place.

d. Edge-Type Loop. The edge-type loop (D) is used on paulins for tieline fastenings. Sometimes it is used as the female half of a toggle fastener. The edge-type loop is made by cutting a piece of webbing double the length of the desired loop. The webbing ends are laid flat with their inner edges touching and their tips alined. The tips are then turned under, and the loop is sewed in place.

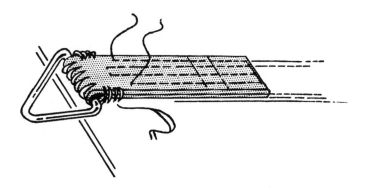

Figure 79. Chape with reinforcement stitching.

a 2-inch-wide strap is about 2½ inches long. Both the inner and outer edges are sewed in place, and an end clip is attached to the raw end.

d. Rolled Loop End. The loop end is rolled as in *c* above, but the end is made only long enough to form a loop for the hardware (C). The end is then looped through the hardware, the raw edge is turned under, and the end is stitched in place.

e. Angled End with Billet. The webbing end is angled (D) by folding in the corners, and a billet is sewed on the angled end.

f. Angled End with Chape. The webbing end is angled as in *e* above, and a chape with hardware is sewed on the angled end.

g. Shaped End with Chape. The webbing end is shaped (E) by cutting a notch in the end of the webbing and bringing the edges of the notch together. A chape with hardware is sewed on the shaped end.

h. Shaped End with Billet. The webbing end is shaped as in *g* above, a billet is placed over the shaped end, a reinforcement strip with raw ends turned under is placed under the shaped end, and the billet and reinforcement strip are sewed in place.

33. Handles

The following types of handles are used in the repair of canvas and webbing items:

a. Plain Webbing Handle. The plain webbing handle (fig 83) is used on carrying cases, bags, and hampers when the strain is carried along the vertical plane of the item. It consists of a single piece of webbing about 12 inches long, twisted into a U-shape, and stitched in place. It is finished with a ½-inch turnunder at the ends and a stitching area approximately 12 inches long (fig 83).

b. Stitched-Grip Webbing Handle. The stitched-grip webbing handle (fig 84) is used on bags and carrying cases when the strain is on the horizontal plane of the item. Procedures for making a common-size stitched-grip handle are as follows:

(1) Cut a 15¼-inch strip of 2-inch-wide heavy cotton webbing, and find the center of the webbing by folding the ends together.

(2) From the center, measure and mark points 2⅞ inches toward each end (A). (These marks indicate the ends of the stitched-grip area of the handle.)

(3) Fold the webbing edges at the stitched-grip area in to the centerline of the webbing, abutting the edges, and stitch them in place.

(4) Double stitch across the grip ends (A).

(5) Cut a duck reinforcement backing 5½ inches wide and 14 inches long.

(6) Center the backing under the area for the handle, turn under the edges one-half inch, and stitch the backing in place (C).

(7) Center the handle on the handle area with a ⅝-inch turnunder at each end and with the ends 12 inches apart, giving slack to the grip section (B).

(8) Stitch the handle in place (A).

(9) From 2-inch-wide webbing, cut two reinforcement pieces 4½ inches long.

(10) Center the reinforcements across the handle ends, turn under the ends of the reinforcements one-half inch, and sew each reinforcement in place (C).

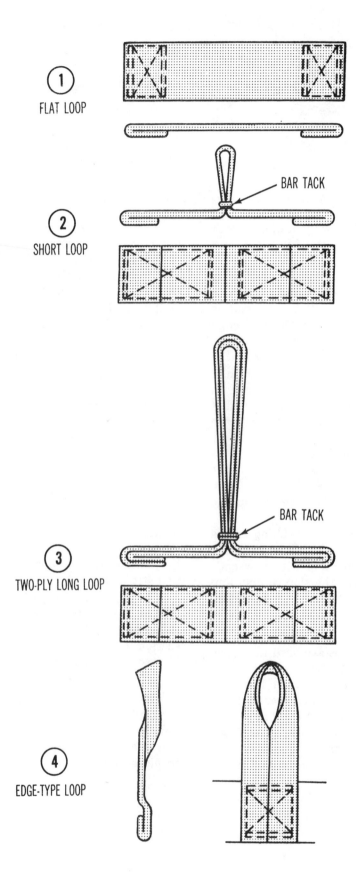

Figure 80. Loop construction.

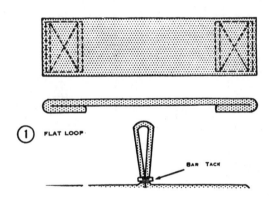

Figure 81. Billet construction.

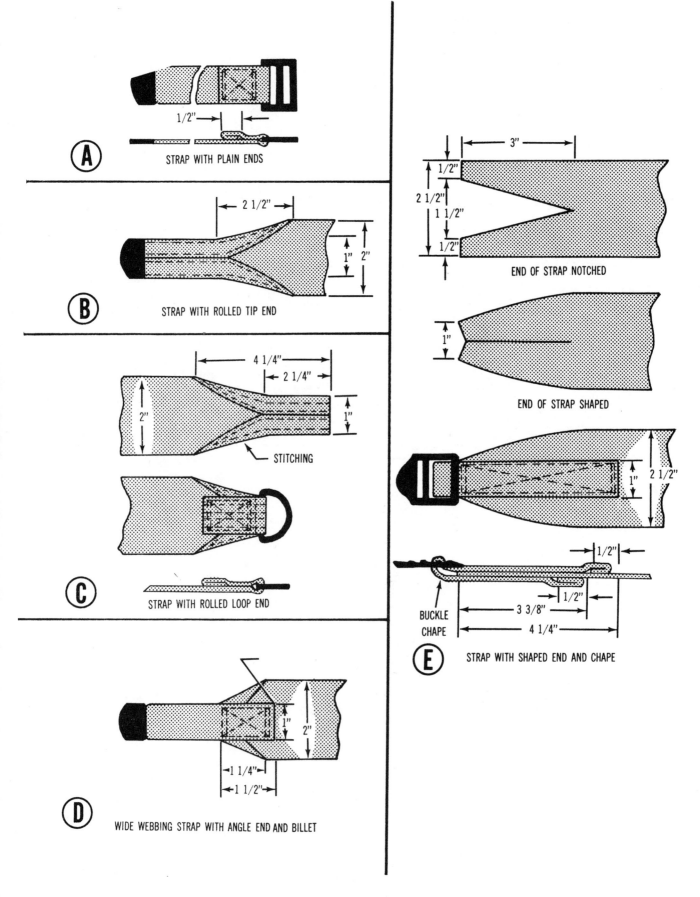

Figure 82. Strap construction.

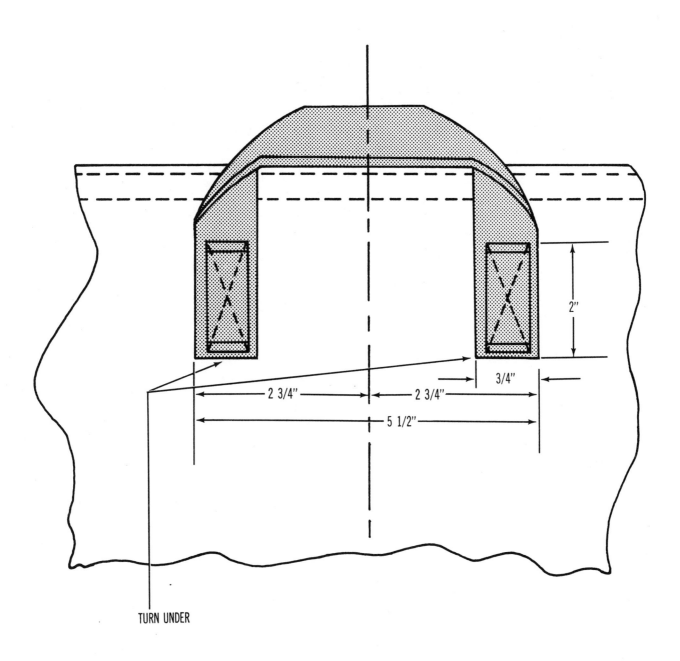

TURN UNDER

Figure 83.   Plain webbing handle.

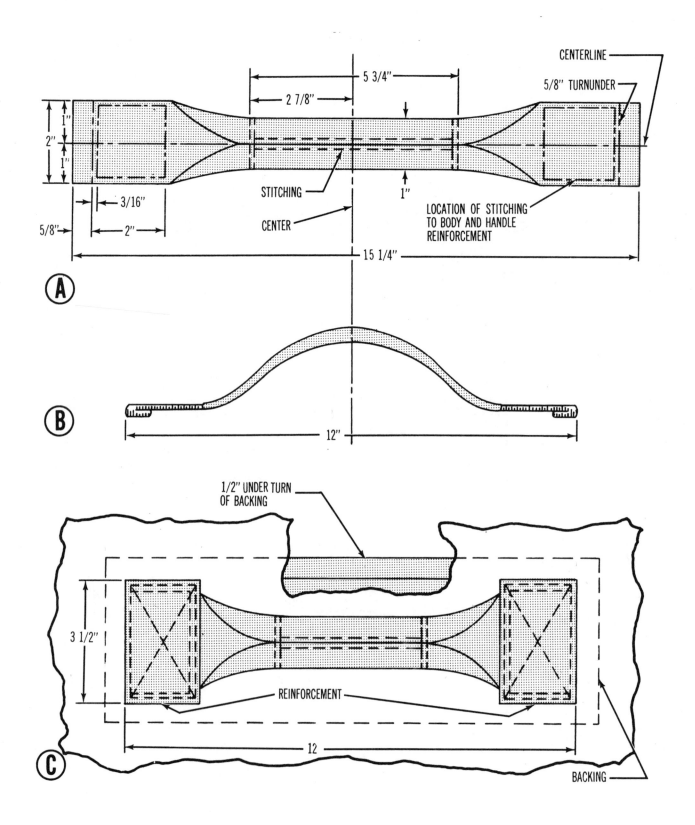

Figure 84. Stitched-grip webbing handle.

34. Stovepipe Openings (fig 85)

Extensive damage to a stovepipe opening is repaired by replacing the opening with a salvaged opening or with a newly fabricated opening. For either replacement, the method of cutting the damaged opening from panel seam to panel seam and sewing the replacement opening to the vent is similar to the method for making the seam-to-seam patch (para 13k), except that the opening is made into the panel replacement before the tent is sewed. Procedures for replacing a stovepipe opening are as follows:

a. Square the damaged opening from seam to seam 2 inches above and below the reinforcement stitches.

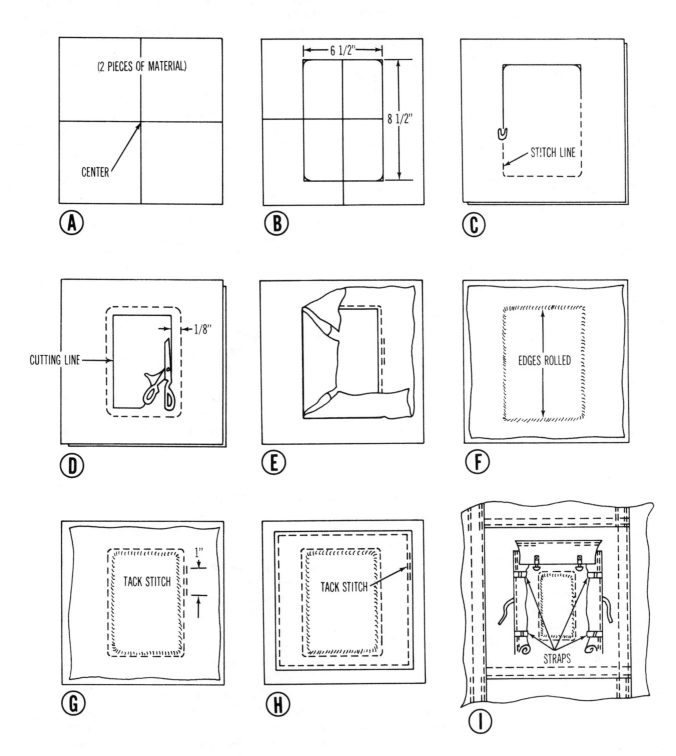

Figure 85. Repair of stovepipe opening.

b. Open the seams within the squared area, and cut out the damaged panel on the marks used to square the panel.

c. Cut the panel replacement as in paragraph 13*k*(4).

d. Cut the reinforcement material the width and length of the reinforcement on the damaged opening, allowing one-half of an inch for turnunder all around the reinforcement piece (A).

e. Mark an outline of the opening on the reinforcement piece, making sure of the exact location and size of the opening (B).

f. Center the reinforcement piece over the panel replacement, with marked outline facing up.

g. Keeping both pieces of material straight and even, sew completely around the marked outline, stitching the two pieces together (C).

h. Cut an opening through both pieces of material, by cutting one-eighth of an inch from the stitches around the inside of the marked outline (D).

i. Tuck the four corners of the reinforcement piece through the opening (E). Turn the pieces over with the reinforcement piece facing down, and pull the corners out square (F).

j. Sew around the opening edge as close as possible without running off the material (G).

k. Fold the reinforcement piece under one-half of an inch, and keeping the material straight and even, stitch around the reinforcement piece, attaching it to the panel (H).

l. Turn the panel over with the reinforcement piece facing down, and replace all flaps and tie ropes according to the construction of the old opening.

m. Stitch the replacement opening to the tent, (I) using the procedure for applying the seam-to-seam patch (para 13*k*).

35. Stovepipe Shields

Extensive damage to a stovepipe shield is repaired by replacing the shield with a salvaged shield or with a new shield. Procedures for repairing tears and holes in the silicone molded shield are as follows:

a. Small Holes and Tears. Small holes and tears 2 inches or less in length may be repaired by spreading silicone sealer (MIL–A–46106) in a layer about 1/16 inch thick on both sides of the shield to bridge across the tear or hole and extend at least 1/2 inch beyond the damaged area in all directions.

(1) Insure that the area to be repaired is clean and dry.

(2) Smooth the sealer, and place the shield so that it does not touch anything.

(3) Allow the sealer to dry 4 to 6 hours. Do not move the tent during the drying period. On bright sunny days of low humidity, allow 4 hours for drying, and on days of high humidity, allow 6 hours.

b. Large Holes and Tears. Large holes and tears can be repaired by using the sealer described in *a* above and a patch made of material salvaged from an unrepairable shield.

(1) Insure that the area to be repaired is clean and dry.

(2) Cut the patch 1 inch larger in all dimensions than the hole or tear.

(3) Apply a layer of sealer on either the patch or the shield, and press the patch in place immediately.

(4) Apply sealer around the edges of the patch 1 inch beyond the damaged area in all directions, and keep the sealed area still for a few hours.

Section VIII. SALVAGE AND FABRICATED PARTS

36. General

Common replacement procedures for many equipment parts are covered earlier in this manual. Many equipment parts, for which there are no common replacement procedures, may also require replacement. These parts should be replaced with salvaged parts when they are at hand. If salvaged parts are not at hand, new parts may be made from patterns.

37. Salvage Parts

When a salvaged part is used for replacement, care should be taken to select a part that matches as closely as possible the color and wear of the item being repaired. Furthermore, since canvas stretches with use, precaution must be taken in sizing.

38. Fabricated Parts

Patterns should be used for fabricating parts from new or salvaged material. If patterns are not at hand, they may be provided in the following ways:

a. Patterns From Old or Damaged Parts. The part to be discarded may be disassembled and used as a pattern. All stitching, hemming, binding, lugs, chapes, and hardware should be removed and the individual pieces opened and laid flat on the material from which the new part is to be made. Because old canvas does not hold its dimensions like a precision-made pattern, it may be necessary to pin the parts before stitching them together.

b. Patterns From Specifications. Specifications are available for canvas and webbing items used in the Army. The specifications give not only the weight of the material, size of thread, length of stitch, size of hardware, and number of parts, but also scale drawings of each component. Specifications for canvas and webbing items may be obtained through channels from US Army Natick Laboratories, Natick, Mass. From specification drawings and dimensions, patterns may be laid out with exactness. Patterns made of pattern material, fiberboard, or sheet metal, if handled properly, insure accurately cut parts and last indefinitely. Typical specification patterns are shown in figure 86.

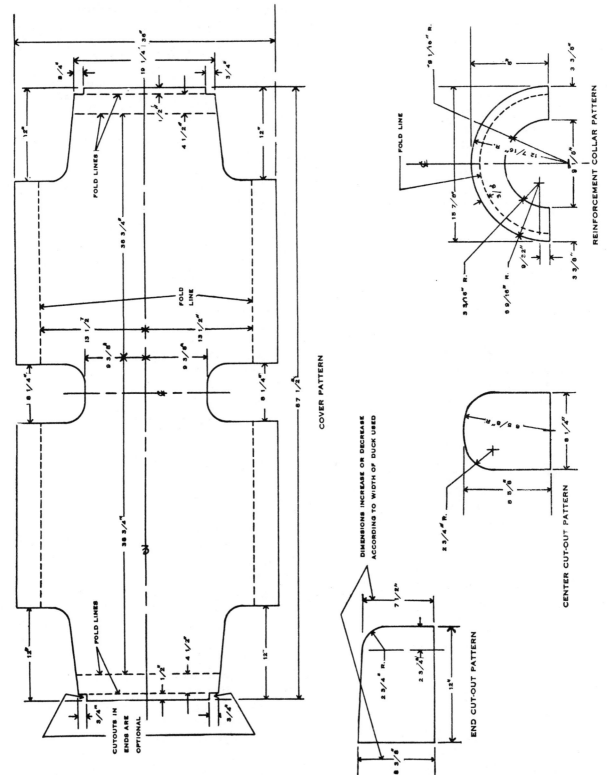

Figure 86. Specification patterns for folding-cot cover.

CHAPTER 5
INSPECTION

Section I.   TENTS AND HEAVY CANVAS

39. Initial Inspection

Before a tent or a heavy canvas item is repaired, it should be given a thorough inspection for defects. Each defect should be marked (para 6) with the appropriate symbol indicating the type of repair required.

a. Tensile Strength. Before suspending a tent or a heavy canvas item for inspection, test the tensile strength of the canvas by grasping a small fold of the canvas between the thumb and forefinger of each hand, gripping it close up so that the tips of the forefingers touch. Tug the canvas several times; if it does not rip, it is repairable as far as its tensile strength is concerned. If it tears on the first try, test several additional areas to learn the extent of the deterioration.

Caution. **When testing, always grasp the canvas against the warp threads, which are the threads running parallel to the selvage. The woof (cross threads), being weak, should not be tugged for testing the tensile strength.**

b. Defects. To inspect a tent or heavy canvas item for defects draw it up by block and tackle. Using the checklist in paragraph 40 as a guide, systematically check for defects, and mark any repairs required (para 6). For inspecting a tent, have one man on the outside do the marking while another man on the inside points out or calls the repairs to be made. Raise the tent a few feet at a time, and check the various parts in the following order:

(1) Peak, or part attached to block and tackle.

(2) Roof.

(3) Eaves.

(4) Side walls.

(5) Sod cloth.

(6) Lines.

(7) Windows.

(8) Screens.

(9) Stovepipe openings.

Note. Check separately such parts as covers, curtains, sashes, ground cloths, and vestibules.

40. Essential Points for Inspection

For inspecting tents and heavy canvas items, use the following checklist as a guide.

a. Canvas.
(1) Tensile strength.
(2) Abrasions.
(3) Holes.
(4) Mildew.
(5) Patches.
(6) Previous repair work.
(7) Seams.
(8) Spots and stains.
(9) Stitching.
(10) Tears.

b. Webbing.
(1) Chapes.
(2) Lines.
(3) Reinforcements.
(4) Straps.
(5) Tapes.

c. Hardware.
(1) Blocks and tackles.
(2) Bull's-eyes.
(3) Chains with plates.
(4) Chains with supporting rings.
(5) End clips.
(6) End hooks.
(7) Eyelets.
(8) Fair-leads.
(9) Fasteners.
(10) Grommets.
(11) Loops.
(12) Plates.
(13) Rings.
(14) D-rings.
(15) Rivets.
(16) S-hooks.
(17) Snaphooks.
(18) Thimbles.
(19) Triangles.
(20) Triangles with hooks.
(21) Wall D-rings.

d. Lines.
(1) Cover.

(2) Door.
(3) Draw.
(4) Eave.
(5) Footstop.
(6) Guy.
(7) Hoisting.
(8) Hood.
(9) Jumper.
(10) Lacing.
(11) Liner-hoisting.
(12) Tie.
(13) Ventilator-flap.
(14) Water-flap.
e. *Unattached Parts.*
(1) Billet.
(2) Covers.
(3) Ground cloths.
(4) Hoods.
(5) Liners.
(6) Sashes.
(7) Shield retainers.
(8) Side walls (canvas and netting).
(9) Tent sections.
(10) Vestibules.

41. Final Inspection

Upon completion of repairs, again inspect the item as in paragraph 39, paying special attention to the quality of the repair work, and make sure of the following:

a. The proper size of thread and length of stitch have been used, and all breaks in the stitching have been backstitched.

b. The stitching has not, through carelessness, fastened together parts that should not be joined.

c. Patches and replaced parts correspond, in color, texture, weight of material, and method of fastening, to the original material and construction of the item.

d. Chapes, loops, and reinforcing strips are of the proper width and length and have been properly stitched.

e. Complementary hardware, such as snap fasteners has been installed to insure perfect engagement without wrinkling or puckering the fabric.

f. Die-inserted hardware, such as snap fasteners and grommet, has been securely clinched without damage to the surrounding fabric.

g. All hardware is of the type and size specified and is in working order.

h. All detached parts, such as curtain liners and sashes, have been checked and are properly attached to the item to which they belong.

Section II. EQUIPMENT OTHER THAN TENTS AND HEAVY CANVAS

42. Initial Inspection

Before each item is repaired, it should be given a thorough inspection for defects. Each defect should be marked (para 6) with the appropriate symbol indicating the type of repair required.

a. Tensile Strength. Before inspecting an item for defects, test the tensile strength of the canvas as in paragraph 39a.

b. Defects. Using the checklist in paragraph 43 as a guide, systematically check the item for defects, and mark any repairs required (para 6). Check the surfaces of the item in the following order:

(1) Top.
(2) Bottom.
(3) Left side.
(4) Right side.
(5) Front.
(6) Back.
(7) Inside.

Note. If an item has several parts, check each part separately, detaching the parts for inspection.

43. Essential Points for Inspection

For inspecting items other than tents and heavy canvas, use the following checklist as a guide:

a. Canvas.
(1) Tensile strength.
(2) Abrasions.
(3) Binding.
(4) Buttonholes.
(5) Hems.
(6) Holes.
(7) Markings.
(8) Mildew.
(9) Seams.
(10) Patches.
(11) Spots and stains.
(12) Stitching.
(13) Tears.
(14) Treatment (waterproofing, fireproofing, and mildew resistance).

b. Hardware.
(1) Buckles.
(2) Buttons.
(3) End clips.
(4) Eyelets.
(5) Fasteners.
(6) Faucets.
(7) Grommets.
(8) Hooks.
(9) Rings.

(10) D-rings.
(11) Rivets.
(12) Snaphooks.
(13) Squares.
(14) Staples.
(15) Tips.
c. *Lines and Tapes.*
(1) Draw.
(2) Lacing.
(3) Tie.
d. *Reinforcements.*
(1) Billet.
(2) Chape.

(3) Grommet.
(4) Handle.
e. *Unattached Parts.*
(1) Covers.
(2) Inserts.
(3) Liners.
(4) Straps.
(5) Suspenders.

44. Final Inspection

Upon completion of repairs, again inspect the Item as in paragraph 42, paying special attention to the quality of the repair work and the conditions listed in paragraph 41*a* through *h*.

Young campers should learn about the qualities of their tenting materials before rigging their shelter. Such information is part of the camping lore taught by the Boy Scouts of America. *(Courtesy of Boy Scouts of America)*

Intrinsic to the maintenance of camping equipment is a knowledge of how the different tenting materials should be handled in varying climes and terrains. Here the Scout arranges for slack in his tent rope in anticipation of a rain storm.
(Courtesy of Boy Scouts of America)

A Scoutmaster instructs the boys in the basic technique of setting up the tent poles in such a way as to stretch the canvas smoothly without making it so tight that it will dislodge tent pegs or damage hardware or fabric under a strain from wind or rain.

(Courtesy of Boy Scouts of America)

Maintenance of camping equipment used in the desert should include daily checks to detect any signs of "cracking" due to the dryness of the climate. *(Courtesy of Boy Scouts of America)*